Cash IN YOUR Coins

2nd Edition
Selling the Rare Coins You've Inherited

BETH DEISHER

FOREWORD BY
Q. DAVID BOWERS

Whitman
Publishing, LLC
PUBLISHING SINCE 1934
www.whitman.com

Cash
IN YOUR Coins

2nd Edition

Selling the Rare Coins You've Inherited

Whitman
Publishing, LLC
PUBLISHING SINCE 1934

www.whitman.com

© 2014 Whitman Publishing, LLC
3101 Clairmont Road, Suite G, Atlanta GA 30329

Correspondence concerning this book may be directed to Whitman Publishing at the address above, attn: Cash In Your Coins.

ISBN 0794842380
Printed in China

This book is designed to provide accurate and authoritative information with regard to the subject matters covered. It is distributed with the understanding that Whitman Publishing and the author are not engaged in rendering legal, financial, or other professional services. If financial or tax advice or other expert professional assistance is required, the services of a competent professional should be sought. The guidance herein is subject to differences of opinion. Before making decisions to buy or sell numismatic collectibles, consult the latest information, including current market conditions. Past performance of the rare-coin market, the bullion market, and commodities markets, or any coin or series within those markets, is not necessarily an indication of future performance, as the future is unknown. Such factors as changing demand, popularity, grading interpretations, strength of the overall market, and national and international economic conditions will continue to be influences.

Whitman Publishing is a leader in the numismatic field. For a catalog of related books, supplies, and storage products, visit Whitman Publishing online at www.Whitman.com, or scan the QR code at left.

CONTENTS

FOREWORD
by Q. David Bowers

What a great book this is! Just think: for less than ten dollars you can profit from Beth Deisher's wisdom gathered over a period of decades. A professional consultation yielding the same information would likely cost many hundreds of dollars and might not be as comprehensive. I do not impress easily, but, wow—this is a book that everyone should own!

Today there are hundreds of fine books to aid those who want to *buy* coins. There are thousands of dealers and millions of coins for sale on the Internet. But when it comes to *selling* coins, information is much harder to find. Truly reliable and unbiased information is very rare.

When you do encounter enticements to sell, they may not be in your best interest. Consider this: you, as an heir or the owner of a family collection, want to obtain as much as you can for your coins, tokens, medals, and paper money. At the same time, buyers want to purchase for the lowest price. I have never seen a buyer who wants to set price records when making offers! Then there are exploitative buyers such as traveling groups who set up in hotels, run splashy advertisements, and offer to buy the public's old coins. I have heard many tales of woe in which coins worth hundreds or thousands of dollars were sold for fractions of their true collector value.

The key to avoiding problems and realizing a fair value is *knowledge*. If you are new to coins—the field of numismatics—you will learn a lot in the pages to follow. The author is not buying coins or selling them, but is sharing her experience and knowledge. As such, her book is unbiased. If you are an established collector and plan to leave your coins to your family or others, the advice given will enable your heirs to learn the real value of what they have. I recommend that you keep a copy of this book among your important papers or with your collection in a safe, bank, or other secure location.

Foreword writer Q. David Bowers, the "Dean of American Numismatics," is the author of more than 50 books. A past president of both the American Numismatic Association and the Professional Numismatists Guild, he serves as research editor of the annual *Guide Book of United States Coins*.

As to my own experience, I have been there and done that. And I am still doing it! I began dealing in coins in 1953 when I was barely a teenager. I fell in love with numismatics, and in time traveled widely, built a fine business, and came to know just about everyone important in the hobby—or, as some call it, the industry. Along the way I served as president of the Professional Numismatists Guild and, later, as president of the American Numismatic Association.

Of the six most valuable collections of American coins ever sold at auction, all were *estate* properties. My company auctioned five of them, including the two most valuable: the John J. Ford Jr. and the Louis E. Eliasberg collections, each of which realized close to $60,000,000. The Harry W. Bass Jr. estate collection realized close to $50,000,000 and was the third most valuable. The fourth was the John J. Pittman estate collection which was handled by David W. Akers. Each of these estate holdings—and I could tell of many others—realized record prices because of careful planning.

More realistically, in terms of your collection and most others the values are not in the tens of millions of dollars, but likely are in the thousands, tens of thousands, or even hundreds of thousands of dollars. Careful planning and analysis will help you or your heirs realize the highest possible price. As Beth Deisher discusses, certain specialties require different methods of sale at auction. A large holding of modern commemorative coins, for example, is sold in a different way than a Proof 1856 Flying Eagle cent worth tens of thousands of dollars. Still another method would be used to sell a "reserve" of gold and silver bullion coins, these being a popular hedge against unexpected political and economic changes. Tokens and medals are yet another field, as is the specialty of paper money.

In a phrase, no one rule fits all.

There are some surprises in this book. Beth shines a light on tax-related questions, suggesting paths to follow and with whom you should consult. For example, it is a common belief that if you "lowball" the value of an inherited coin you will minimize taxes. Beth explains that this can lead to significantly *higher* taxes once the coin is sold! She breaks down estate taxes and other legal concepts in easy-to-understand language, illustrating them with real-world examples.

If you are already an experienced collector but are seeking estate advice, you will learn a lot. In other areas, you will find useful information on, for example, every coin type the U.S. Mint has ever made. Bookmark chapter 5 with a note to your heirs! This chapter alone could protect them from selling a valuable coin for a giveaway price.

Case studies offer illustrations and walk you through the process of identifying your coins, building an inventory on paper or by computer, figuring out coin values, and making the most money from selling.

I've known Beth Deisher for many years. It was back in 1961 that Margo Russell, an early editor of *Coin World*, asked me to write a weekly column. Today "The Joy of Collecting" is still one of the best-read features in this publication. When Margo retired in 1985, Beth took over the editorial reins at *Coin World*. From then until 2012 she was anywhere and everywhere in the hobby. As editor of the world's most popular and most-used numismatic publication it was her challenge, working with a fine staff, to keep on top of events, trends, and other information. This meant studying the market and its changes, keeping abreast of constantly changing taxes and regulations, and knowing the field of professional numismatics inside and out.

During that time we communicated constantly. I helped with many questions and situations, and wrote well over a thousand weekly columns. I saw Beth in action at coin conventions and public ceremonies, weighing in on legal situations, giving congressional testimony, and more. She contributed to books and started new magazines. Along the way she has given many programs and presentations, ranging from popular subjects to esoteric—the latter including a detailed seminar on detecting sophisticated and deceptive counterfeit coins. Remarkable! I daresay that it would be hard to ask Beth Deisher a question about buying, selling, or maximizing your security and returns that she could not answer.

With this book you are, in effect, sitting down with Beth Deisher in your living room or office, perhaps over coffee, and talking about coins.

With her friendly guidance and expertise you're sure to avoid costly mistakes, find the greatest value in your coin collection, and feel comfortable and secure with your newfound knowledge. You'll make decisions about your coins with more confidence. You'll sleep better knowing that a uniquely qualified friend has shared decades of personal and professional experience. Enjoy the conversation—and profit from it!

Q. David Bowers
Wolfeboro, New Hampshire

PREFACE

A few months after becoming editor of *Coin World* in 1985, I answered my phone at work one morning and heard a woman's voice proclaiming, almost in a demanding voice, "I need to know what to do with these coins."

Before I could finish saying "*Coin World* is a weekly publication. We do not buy or sell—," she cut me off.

"I know *Coin World* is a publication," she said. "And you're the editor, right?"

A little stunned, and certainly intrigued, I acknowledged: "Yes, I'm the editor." And then asked, "So how can I help you?"

"Well, I certainly need help," she said. But this time her voice was mellow, almost apologetic. "You probably think I'm crazy. But I just didn't know who else to call." And then she began to share her story.

Her husband of 28 years had died suddenly about a year earlier. He had been a coin collector since childhood. They had had a modest but good life. He had worked for the same company all of his working years. She had worked two jobs in recent years to help pay off the mortgage.

After her husband died, she found some silver dollars and some Wheat pennies in a small safe in their home and assumed that was his collection. She had never been interested in coins and had never really talked about coins with him.

Within the past month, payment-due notices for safety deposit boxes, addressed to her husband, had arrived in the mail. There were seven, all from banks within an hour's drive. Upon receiving the first notice, she had thought there must be a mix-up. But as she received more and began to check with the various banks, she found that her husband had rented the safety deposit boxes for many years. She searched her house and to her surprise found an envelope containing seven keys identified by bank. Visits to each bank revealed safety deposit boxes filled with gold coins.

"I don't know a thing about coins. I don't know who to talk to. In fact, I'm scared to tell anybody that I even have these gold coins!" she admitted. "But I know my husband trusted you folks at *Coin World*, so I sat down and looked through the issue that came in the mailbox yesterday. And I found your name and *Coin World*'s phone number."

Of course, the world technologically was much different then. In 1985 professional third-party grading services did not exist. The Internet as the public has come to use it today was more than a decade away. The most readily available tool was the venerable "Red Book," which I suggested she use to identify the coins and create an inventory list. After completing the inventory, she called to say that she had found a receipt from an auction house. Aware that sometimes coin dealers work with clients in building collections, I suggested that she call the well-known firm. A day later she called back to tell me that she had talked with a member of the staff who was aware of her husband's collection. Later she consigned the gold coins for auction, and they were sold over a three-year period. After the final auction she shared that while she would now have a very comfortable retirement, she wished that he had "just once told me about them!"

While not everyone who has reached out to me learned that they had inherited coins of great value, their stories have been remarkably similar. They knew very little about the coins that had been passed down to them and they were apprehensive about selling them, fearing that they would be "taken" by buyers. The advice I gave to the gold-coin collector's wife provided the concept for this book. The ability to help her and many others throughout the years inspired me to put all of that information and more into a single concise and convenient form.

The first edition of *Cash In Your Coins: Selling the Rare Coins You've Inherited* was published in June of 2013. Since then, I have traveled extensively throughout the United States presenting educational forums and doing book signings. The number and value of the coins and numismatic collectibles might differ, but it seems as though almost every family has a stash of "old coins" that has been passed down through the family! Inevitably, they have procrastinated learning more or doing anything with the coins, fearing the unknown. It's time to shed the fear. Use the information in this book to confidently identify, value, and reap the benefits of your inheritance!

Beth Deisher

There is one essential question you must be able to answer before selling your coins and other numismatic collectibles. Explore why finding the answer is the key to success. Also learn the one thing you should never do to a coin or any numismatic collectible.

CAN YOU ANSWER THIS QUESTION?

"How much do you want for your coins?"

That's the first question any buyer will ask when you have coins or any such collectible items (paper money, tokens, medals, etc.) to sell. If you do not know their current value, you are at a disadvantage.

If you did not personally collect or accumulate the coins and know little about them, you are doubly disadvantaged.

The goal of this book is to help move you from "disadvantaged" to being a knowledgeable and confident seller. The information herein will help you identify what you have, estimate a current market value, and explore the various options open to you as a seller.

This book deals with coins produced in the United States. However, the fundamentals of handling, storing, and protecting your coins are basically the same, regardless of where they were manufactured. Identifying, valuing, and selling *non*-U.S. items differs. Information suggesting sources and references for non-U.S. material is provided in chapter 8.

DIFFERENT KINDS OF COIN COLLECTORS

Typically family members or friends receive coins as gifts or inherit them from a collector. There are various types of collectors:

Accumulator. An accumulator saves coins or monetary instruments in a random fashion. Often the accumulation is a hoard of a particular denomination. For example, there is a perception within the general public that "Wheaties" or Lincoln cents (commonly referred to as pennies) with the "Wheat ears" reverse (produced from 1909 through 1958) are rare and valuable. Many people throughout the years have hoarded them by the thousands or even tens of thousands—in barrels, in buckets, in large bags, etc. Some Wheaties are rare because of low survival rates for a specific year and mintmark, die variety, or error type. However, the

The coins you inherit might be carefully sorted and cataloged, or they might be jumbled together in piles.

majority are not rare and do not carry a significant collector premium. Wheaties, like cents with the Memorial reverse produced from 1959 through 1981, are made of 95 percent copper. Since it is illegal to melt U.S. one-cent coins for their copper value, two options are open (beyond taking them to your local bank for face value). The first is to sell to dealers or collectors, who may pay a slight premium for the opportunity to search large quantities for rarities. The second option has materialized since the price of copper began to escalate in early 2004. Traders on eBay buy and sell large quantities of 95 percent copper cents based on the market price of copper. Since coins gathered or saved by accumulators are usually unsorted, unclassified, and unattributed, selling in bulk is a good strategy if you do not have the time to search the accumulation to find those that have a collector premium. See chapter 5 for more information.

Coins gathered by an *accumulator* (as opposed to a collector or numismatist) might be found stacked in piles, dumped into cigar boxes, and hoarded in bags, tins, and storage bins.

Casual collector. The majority of people in the United States who describe themselves as coin collectors casually collect coins in a variety of ways. They "save back" from circulation coins that are new or of interest to them. For example, many people in the mid-1960s saved 90 percent silver dimes, quarters, and half dollars as the U.S. Mint began issuing "clad" coins (of the same denominations but made of copper and nickel). They did not save particular dates or even denominations. They just kept any coins with silver in them with the thought that some day they would be worth more than face value. In more recent times, as Congress has approved coinage programs designed to provide new designs for U.S. circulating coins, many Americans eagerly looked forward to the release of each quarter in the 10-year 50 State Quarters® Program that began in 1999 and ended in 2008. Most people were satisfied to find one example of each quarter in circulation. Others sought examples issued by both mints that produced the quarters for circulation, Philadelphia and Denver. Many of these collectors, as they located examples, filled in quarter boards or albums designed specifically for the State quarters. Many also ordered from the U.S. Mint special collector versions (in Mint and Proof sets) of the five coins issued each year during the program. All of these coin-collecting activities were pursued for fun, without regard for the grade of the individual coins and/or potential for future value. Casual collectors usually do not take the time to set up an inventory of their holdings or keep records of their purchases.

Numismatist. Often described as a "serious" or "advanced" collector, a numismatist is highly knowledgeable about the history and science of coinage. Numismatists can be generalists with broad interests, or specialists who focus their study, research, and collecting in particular series or denominations. Most numismatists set collecting goals, such as completing a set of a design series or all coins of a particular denomination at a certain grade level. Some numismatists pursue collecting for the fun of the "chase of the hunt." Others lean more toward the investment side, viewing their collection as a store of value in addition to being a rewarding endeavor. In general, most numismatists maintain an inventory of their collection(s) and are meticulous record keepers with regard to acquisition costs and the pedigree or ownership history (if known) of their coins. The key word here is *most*. Some numismatists are averse to recordkeeping, preferring to keep all of the information about their coins and collection(s) "in their heads." That's fine, when the numismatist is alive and well and able to take charge of dispersing the collection, whether by selling it or giving it to others or donating it to a museum.

WHAT TO DO IF THERE'S NO INVENTORY

Problems arise when the owner or the person who collected the coins— whether he was an accumulator, casual collector, or numismatist—is not available, and no instructions or inventory exist. (Incidentally, it is entirely realistic to reference the collector as *he*. Research by numismatic organizations and numismatic publications indicates that in the United States 90

A numismatist often will keep careful records of his coin collection, noting when his coins were purchased, where, and for what price. He might use a computer spreadsheet, or handwritten notes, or a ledger like the *Check List and Record Book of United States and Canadian Coins* (pictured).

to 93 percent of coin collectors are men. [This is likely true in other nations as well.] While the percentage may change in the future, coin collecting is and has been the domain of the male gender. Thus the collection you have received and need to find out more information about was likely gathered or collected by a husband, a father, a grandfather, a brother, a son, or an uncle, or by multiple generations of males in a family.)

Of course, there's also the possibility that you have discovered a coin or coins as a result of treasure hunting with a metal detector or found a stash of coins in some unlikely place, such as in the walls of an old house or in the rafters of an old building.

Regardless of the source, identifying the coins and developing an inventory—especially if you are dealing with coins in an estate—is the essential first step. However, there are practical considerations and things to do before beginning the inventory. *There is also one very important thing that you should **not** do.*

NEVER clean a coin!

One of the greatest temptations, upon seeing coins that have been stored for a long time, is to "clean" them or to make them shiny—especially silver coins.

The best advice is to *never* attempt to clean a coin! This is especially true if you have little to no experience in handling coins. Most forms of cleaning—wiping, polishing, buffing, rinsing with soap and water, or immersing in a bath of soda water—can damage the surface of a coin or remove microscopic layers of the metal. These forms of cleaning leave very light scratches called *hairlines*, which greatly reduce the collector value of a coin.

Experts who possess the knowledge and skill to remove dirt and undesirable residue on a coin's surface without damaging the coin can "properly" clean some coins. If you encounter a "dirty" coin or one that is tarnished but you think may be of significant value, set it aside or place it in a holder and let the experts deal with it later.

Over time all metals react with oxygen and other elements in the environment. A common term for oxidation is *tarnish*. The coin collecting community uses a gentler word: *toning*. Visually pleasing toning, especially on silver coins, appeals to some collectors and they will some-times pay extra for "original" toning—considered to be the result of natural processes over time. ("Artificial toning" or coloration induced by human intervention using a variety of methods and chemicals is not desirable and is a deceptive practice, usually employed to hide a scratch or some other form of damage on the coin's surface.)

This 1878-S Morgan dollar, auctioned by Stack's Bowers Galleries in 2011, was praised for its original toning. "Teal, lemon, and russet hues grace the obverse in delicate appeal," noted the auction catalog, "while the reverse is toned at the rims but with deeper jewel tones of blue, purple, and russet-gold with the center still bright silver." (shown enlarged)

Meanwhile, this 1886-O Morgan dollar was noted in the auction catalog to have "questionable color"—meaning it might be artificially toned. "Both sides are vividly toned," the auction description observed, "the obverse in mottled rose and powder-blue patina and the reverse with even reddish-gold iridescence."

Exposure to sulfur, especially on silver coins, results in a very thin (25 to 125 nanometers) film of sulfide on the surface of the coin. The thinnest film is light yellow in color. With longer exposure to sulfur, the film gets thicker and changes to a golden yellow, then red, then purple, then blue, and finally dark grey or black. Often the surface of one side of the coin is exposed at different rates and it is possible to see three or more of the colors—gold, red, purple, and blue—on various sections of the coin's surface at the same time. Collectors often refer to this as *rainbow toning*. It is possible that one side of a silver coin exhibits toning and the other side is "white," virtually free of toning. If a coin has been partially covered by another coin or some other object, only the part of the coin that was exposed shows toning. Copper is also highly susceptible to toning. Newly struck copper coins are red-orange in color. (Collectors prize copper coins that exhibit brilliant red-orange surfaces and refer to them as "red.") As copper oxidizes and reacts with elements in the environment its color turns to brown. Depending on the alloy (the amount of copper and other metals in the planchet), a coin with lesser amounts of copper may exhibit a greyish brown or even green color after prolonged exposure to oxygen and other elements. The nobler precious metals that you are likely to encounter with coins, such as gold and platinum, are less susceptible to toning.

Copper coins can vary in color from original mint red to various shades of chocolate brown. (shown enlarged)

OLD-FASHIONED WAYS OF COIN STORAGE

Before the invention and widespread use of today's chemically inert plastic holders, coins were stored in a variety of ways. Virtually all older storage methods exposed coins to sulfur compounds, either in a solid or gaseous state. Wood contains sulfur and many coins toned from having been stored in dresser drawers or even specially made wooden coin cabinets. Most paper contains sulfur, thus coins stored in paper envelopes, cardboard coin boards and albums, cigar boxes, cardboard boxes used by the U.S. Mint, or paper wrappers were exposed to sulfur. Even original canvas and cloth bags used by the Mint and banks contained some sulfur.

If you encounter coins stored in small, brown envelopes with writing on them, be sure to keep the envelopes because they may contain important information, such as the price at acquisition or a note with regard to rarity. Even if you transfer the coin to a different holder, keep the envelope and reference it in the inventory.

Likewise, you may find notations on the outside of wrappers used to house rolls of coins. If the coins are in original bank or U.S. Mint wrappers, do not remove them from the wrapper because there is a collector premium for original (untouched since being minted), unsearched rolls of coins. List such rolls in your inventory as original and note the denomination, year, and mintmark (if visible from the coins at the ends of the rolls), and total face value.

Original rolls of new coins are wrapped at coin terminals, which are private facilities contracted by the Federal Reserve and the U.S. Mint. Bank-wrapped rolls of each denomination of new coins are tightly wrapped in paper wrappers that are crimped at each end, with most of the obverse or reverse of the coins at each end showing. Each wrapper states the denomination and the total face value of coins contained within the roll. The jagged seam on the side of the paper wrapper identifies an original bank-wrapped roll. Original rolls before the 1970s have distinctive colors for each denomination.

Paper wrappers with one end crimped can today be purchased from retailers, and crimpers (easily available in the retail market) can be used to close the open end. However, the seam on the side of these wrappers is straight (as opposed to jagged) and the rolls are not as tightly wrapped as original bank-wrapped rolls. Paper wrappers with ends folded are used to store and sort coins. Often you will find that the person who wrapped such rolls wrote on the outside of the wrapper information about the contents—for example, if the roll contains coins of the same

If the collector saved receipts and invoices, keep them handy. Those kinds of records can be useful in valuing your coins.

Old envelopes and paper wrappers can reveal useful information about a coin's history.

year and mintmark. It is advisable to open any rolls that have been privately wrapped to verify the count of coins, their conditions, and the date and mintmarks of coins within the roll.

In the late 1990s, some coin terminals began using clear plastic to house rolls of coins. Such rolls do not have seams, and heat is used to

Coin boards, folders, and albums have been popular for storage and display since the 1930s.

Coins used to be shipped and stored in canvas bags. These are sometimes still seen today.

make the ends of the roll tighter. Original, new rolls of coins can be found in clear plastic wrappers. But it is also possible to find in clear plastic "mixed" rolls that contain both new and circulated coins. Since the plastic is clear, you can count the number of coins in the roll.

Prior to the advent of 2-by-2–inch plastic holders, many collectors used 2-by-2 cardboard holders with clear windows. Two pieces of the cardboard holders were stapled together with the coin in the center of the window so that both sides of the coin could be viewed. Collectors often made notes on the cardboard portion, such as denomination, mintmark, acquisition price, and other information. Unless there is rust on the staples or the window has been torn, keep the coins in the 2-by-2 cardboard holders.

If the coins are in albums, keep them in the original album. Many coin boards and cardboard folders have slots for each date and mintmark

Cardboard holders, two inches square and with a clear window, are popular among coin collectors. Handwritten or typed notations can provide valuable information about the coins they hold.

as well as for some popular die varieties. Such holders typically were filled with the obverse (or "heads") side of the coin showing. With most coins, you will be able to determine the date and mintmark by looking at the obverse side. Unless you need to take the coin out of the album to inspect the reverse (or "tails") side, leave it in the album. The less the coin is handled, the smaller likelihood of damage to the coin.

Coin albums available during the last 30 years typically have holes in the cardboard but also have plastic covers that slide through each row to protect the coins from falling out and also to allow inspecting both the obverse and reverse of the coin. Unless there is some reason to take a coin out, leave it in the album.

Coins and coin sets in U.S. Mint packaging are best left in the original packaging. This might include cellophane "blister" packs or plastic cases. The blister packs and plastic cases might be housed in boxes that you may need to open in order to verify that the set is complete. Mint-produced sets state the year of issue, the issuing authority (U.S. Mint), and what the product is—such as *Mint set*, *Proof set*, or the name of the set if associated with a special program.

Some of today's coin albums have plastic slides that protect coins and allow them to be displayed front and back.

PROFESSIONALLY "SLABBED" COINS

Professional coin-grading firms began using sonically sealed plastic holders in 1986. After they grade the coin, they encase it in a rectangular, rigid plastic tamper-proof holder commonly referred to as a *slab*. An insert at the top of the slab identifies the coin by denomination, date, mintmark, and grade (state of preservation) on a 70-point scale. The slab will also carry the name and logo of the grading service. There have been dozens of grading services to enter the market since 1986, so you could encounter a slab issued by a grading service that is no longer in business. However, do not attempt to remove the coin from the slab, because it contains important information about the coin. It also provides good protection from damage for the coin. The plastic used for these slabs does "breathe," which means that slabs do not provide absolute protection from the environment. Depending on where the slab may have been stored and how long it has been stored, a coin encapsulated in a slab may exhibit toning. Because of the expense of the fees charged to grade and encapsulate a coin, generally only coins valued at $100 or more are more likely to reside in slabs.

With the advent of professional paper-money–grading services within the first five years of the 21st century, paper money began to be graded and encapsulated in holders made of archival-quality inert clear semi-rigid plastic material, which allows you to see both sides of the note. As with coins, the more valuable notes are likely to be in professional grading-service holders due to the costs of grading. If you find paper money in such holders, do not attempt to remove the notes. The information and protection afforded by the holders will greatly assist you and help preserve the notes' quality.

Professional third-party grading services encapsulate coins in tamper-resistant plastic "slabs" with their grades noted.

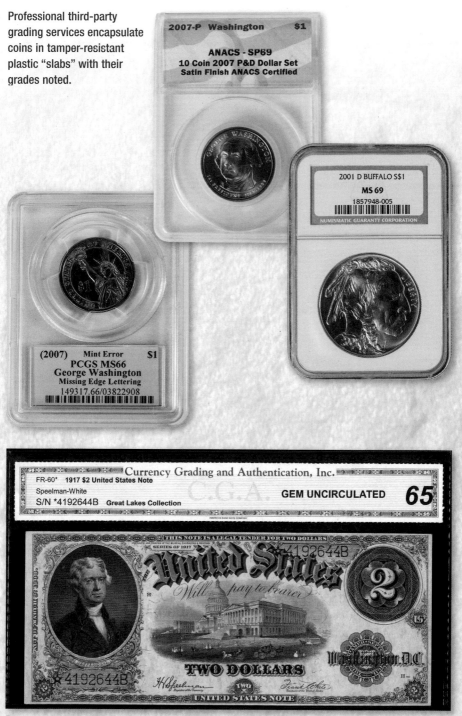

2007-P Washington $1

ANACS - SP69
10 Coin 2007 P&D Dollar Set
Satin Finish ANACS Certified

2001 D BUFFALO S$1
MS 69
1857948-005
NUMISMATIC GUARANTY CORPORATION

(2007)   Mint Error $1
PCGS MS66
George Washington
Missing Edge Lettering
149317.66/03822908

Currency Grading and Authentication, Inc.
FR-60* 1917 $2 United States Note
Speelman-White
S/N *4192644B   Great Lakes Collection
C.G.A.   GEM UNCIRCULATED   65

Paper money, too, can be slabbed by the professional grading services.

2

PREPARING TO LOOK AT YOUR COINS

Throughout this book our first reference will be to coins. However, many accumulations and collections contain paper money and other related money items such as tokens and medals. In general, medals and tokens are like coins, so the tools and methods of handling them are the same. There are slight variances for paper money, as discussed in this chapter.

One of your first considerations regarding the items in your custody is to make sure they remain in the same state of preservation or condition as when you received them. Improper handling and storage can be very costly.

TOOLS YOU WILL NEED

☐ **A table or desk in a room or secure place that has adequate space for you to spread out the coins and be comfortable as you examine them.** If the collection contains a number of coins, you might

One "must" is making sure your coins and other numismatic collectibles are not damaged due to improper handling. Focus on the tools you will need, and how to use them, as well as tips for handling coins and paper money.

not be able to complete your work in one sitting or a few hours. For security, it is desirable to be able to close or lock the room and return when you have time to resume working with the coins. *Also, the fewer people who know that you are working with the collection, the better, especially if you are working with the coins in your home. If there is a chance that others will have access to the room or space, plan to work on small portions at a time, and at the end of a work session return the coins to a safe container and place it in a secure location.* If you're working at home, it is advisable to select a workspace that is a low-traffic area and off limits to children and pets. If the room has windows, it is best to keep the blinds closed or drapes drawn while working with the coins and paper money.

☐ **Soft cloth to cover a portion of the top of your desk or work-table.** A swath (14 by 9 inches or slightly larger) of inexpensive velvet or velveteen cloth should be used much like a placemat to cover the space on the table surface where you will be examining the coins. The soft

Your work station is very important and should be planned in advance.

cloth will protect the coins should you inadvertently drop them. Dropping a coin on a hard wooden, metal, or glass surface could irrevocably damage it. Coin dealers often use a "coin pad," which is a 13.5 by 8.75–inch stiff piece of cardboard covered in black velveteen. It is not necessary to purchase a coin pad since you can make your own using a small piece of cloth from your local fabric store. Some collectors spread several layers of newspapers and then cover the area with felt or velvet cloth in order to provide a cushion for the working surface. An inexpensive (under $5) alternative to making your own cushion is purchasing a 100-percent polyester 18 by 16–inch dish-drying mat in the housewares section of stores that sell kitchen items. Be sure to use the mat exclusively for examining your numismatic collectibles, in order to avoid any chemicals or other contaminants. By using a protective cloth or mat you can avoid dings, bumps, and scratches to a coin's surface, if the coin is dropped or otherwise mishandled.

A padded surface protects coins from accidental damage from dropping.

An inexpensive dish-drying mat can serve the purpose.

☐ **A magnifying glass.** If you have excellent vision, you might not need a magnifying glass. An important step in identifying coins is locating the mark or letter designating the mint that manufactured the coin. Mint-marks tend to be the smallest letters or symbols on a coin. If you decide to use a magnifying glass, you do not need an expensive one. A hand-held magnifier with 5-power magnification is sufficient. Magnifying glasses for viewing two-inch and smaller areas are available at office-supply stores and hobby or coin shops. Dealers and collectors who examine lots of coins often use 7- to 10-power magnification. Much depends on your eyesight and how much you want to spend on tools for this project. A good test to determine whether you need a magnifying glass is to take a dime out of your pocket or pocketbook; can you easily read the date and all other words and letters on both sides of the coin? If you find yourself squinting or unsure of the numbers or letters/words, a magnifying glass is warranted.

☐ **Good lighting.** Sunlight through a window is not likely to be sufficient illumination for examining coins. You will need good overhead lighting as well as a good source of focused light, such as a desk or table-top lamp. Professional graders and coin dealers often shut out sunlight, suggesting it may distort the color of a coin's surface. Halogen lamps are recommended for examining paper money. Take care that you do not leave paper money in direct sunlight because it can cause the images to fade, and prolonged exposure makes paper yellow and brittle.

☐ **Gloves.** Gloves are optional. Many collectors and coin dealers handle hundreds or thousands of coins without using gloves. However, gloves offer a measure of protection—especially important if you expect to be holding rare and valuable coins or paper money. Coins, medals, and paper money should be held by their edges. Human skin contains acids and other naturally occurring chemicals. Thus your fingertips can leave residue on a coin's surface that does not go away and cannot be removed without damaging the coin. The same contaminants can also harm paper money. White cotton gloves that fit all sizes can be purchased at hobby and coin shops, or online from sellers of hobby-supply items. Usually gloves are sold in pairs and can be purchased in bulk lots. If you expect to be handling lots of coins and decide to use gloves, purchasing several pair would be a good option. Gloves are also recommended for handling paper money. White cotton gloves or disposable nitrile gloves are best. (Nitrile is a type of synthetic rubber. It contains no latex proteins.)

☐ **A cloth, surgical, or paper dust mask.** A mask is optional. It acts a barrier between the moisture in your breath and the surface of the coin or paper money. Moisture can cause spots on the metal of a coin's surface. Such spots can damage and greatly devalue your coins. If you do not use a mask, avoid talking while examining coins or paper money. Saliva droplets from your mouth can land on a coin's surface and cause permanent damage to the coin. Also, avoid eating and drinking while examining coins or paper money. It you need a refreshment break, move

Gloves are handy for protecting your coins during inspection; pictured are white cotton and nitrile examples. A face mask can also be helpful for keeping respiratory moisture off the coins.

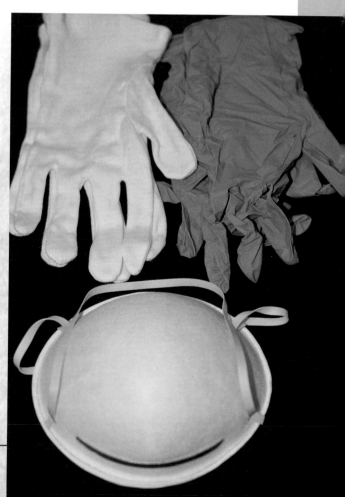

away from the desk or table in the work area, and drink or eat at a distance. Before returning to the work area, wash your hands in hot soapy water and dry thoroughly.

☐ **Holders.** As you identify coins and paper money that have collector value, you will need to separate them and store them in holders, tubes, or albums to protect them from damage. There are several types and brands available from hobby and coin shops. You can also purchase them online from vendors selling coin / paper money supplies. They are usually listed under "storage."

One of the most popular brands and types of holders for coins is the Saflip® 2-by-2–inch clear plastic holder that consists of two pockets that fold in the center. One pocket holds the coin; the other pocket holds a paper insert on which to record information about the coin. (Never store a coin in each pocket of the holder and take the risk of damaging the coins.) The holder is made of inert polyethylene terephthalate and contains no oils or PVC (polyvinyl chloride; see next page).

Flexible, foldable plastic flips, commonly measuring 2 by 2 inches, can be used to store individual valuable coins.

Cardboard 2-by-2 holders with DuPont Mylar® windows or polyester film windows are also popular and quite economical. Some brands are self-adhesive and others require the cardboard to be stapled to ensure the coin will not drop out. The windows are sized for various coin denominations.

Clear-plastic capsules are another option for storing individual coins. These consist of a top and bottom that fit together snugly or screw together to enclose the coin.

Regardless of the brand or type (flips or capsules) you choose, make sure the plastic does not contain PVC (polyvinyl chloride). Many plastic holders and sheets with coin / paper money pockets sold in the 1960s and 1970s contained PVC. Over time this particular plastic reacts with the metal in a coin, producing a green film and spotting. Experts can remove the green film and spots, but the corrosive damage from PVC is irreparable. PVC holders are softer and more pliable than safer plastics (such as Mylar®); a safer, non-corrosive flip usually is brittle and stiffer than PVC.

Cowens 2-by-2 coin holders use a patent-coated board lined with extra-heavy DuPont Mylar® as a non-reactive protective lining for coins. These can be purchased in economically in bundles of 100.

The various brands of 2-by-2 holders can be purchased in bulk lots, with or without storage boxes. If it is likely that you will need more than 50, it pays to buy in quantity, especially when purchasing online from coin-supply retailers.

If you have a large number of coins of a particular denomination, coin tubes may be a good storage option. Look for inert polystyrene coin tubes. The size and the number of coins each tube holds depend on the denomination. Coin tubes are usually sold in bulk and they are fairly inexpensive.

Larger holders are made to house paper money of various sizes. They, too, should not contain any PVC. Paper-money specialists recommend Mylar® (polyester-film) holders. If you elect to purchase albums in which to place the coins or paper money, make sure the albums are acid free and that any holders or slides used to secure coins are PVC free.

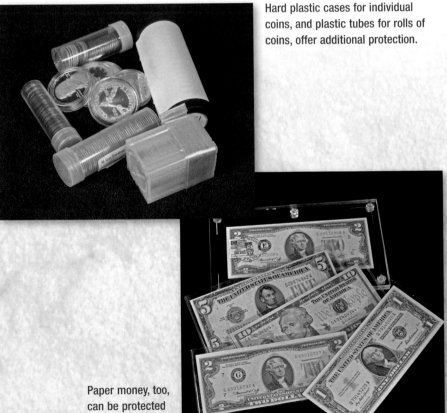

Hard plastic cases for individual coins, and plastic tubes for rolls of coins, offer additional protection.

Paper money, too, can be protected and displayed in special holders.

☐ **A coin price guide.** The most widely available retail price guide for U.S. coins is *A Guide Book of United States Coins*, by R.S. Yeoman, edited by Kenneth Bressett. It is widely referred to as the "Red Book" due to its color. The Red Book has been published annually since 1946 and carries an advance year date. (The first edition, published in November 1946, was given a cover date of 1947. Since it is published annually, the year is part of the title. Thus in mid-2016 it will be possible to purchase the 2017 Red Book.) It contains complete listings and retail pricing information for all U.S. coins produced since 1792 to the year the book was published. The Red Book also contains sections on pre-federal issues (colonial and post-colonial coins and tokens that circulated in the New World before the Philadelphia Mint began operation), commemorative coins, Proof sets and Mint sets, U.S. bullion coins produced since 1986, significant U.S. pattern coins, and privately issued coins and tokens. The Red Book is available in most bookstores, coin shops, and hobby centers. It can also be purchased online, including directly from the publisher, Whitman Publishing (www.Whitman.com). The spiral-bound softcover version is handy for inventory purposes. (Other formats include hardcover, spiral-bound hardcover, perfect-bound softcover, and a Large Print version.) A continuously updated online version of the Red Book is available in digital format by subscription (www.RedBookOnline.com).

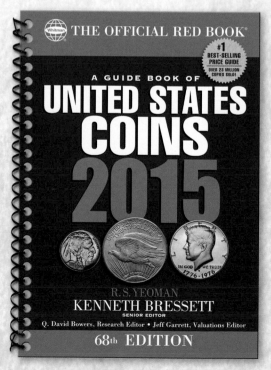

A price guide, such as the annually issued *Guide Book of United States Coins* (the "Red Book") is a necessary tool as you inventory your coins.

If a significant quantity of U.S. paper money is among the items you need to inventory and wish to sell, it would be advisable to also purchase a paper-money guide. Whitman publishes such references for various levels of hobby interest: general (*A Guide Book of United States Currency* by Kenneth Bressett), intermediate (the *Guide Book of U.S. Paper Money* by Arthur and Ira Friedberg), and advanced (the *Whitman Encyclopedia of U.S. Paper Money* by Q. David Bowers). Other price guides are available on the newsstand and in bookstores, such as *Coin World*'s monthly special-edition magazine, which contains listings for U.S. coins and paper money.

☐ **A grading guide.** Since the condition or state of preservation (most often referred to as the *grade*) of a coin or piece of paper money is a key factor in determining its value, you will need to have a basic understanding of grading and a grading guide to assist you. If you have a lot of coins to inventory and sell, it will pay to purchase a grading guide. There are a number of grading guide books available for U.S. coins. One grading guide is sufficient. Among those recommended are:

- *Coin World's Making the Grade,* by Beth Deisher. This large-format (8-1/2 by 11-inch) softcover book provides enlarged color images in a wide range of grades for each U.S. coin series as well as color maps that show the areas on each side of the coin where surface imperfections most affect the grade. It also includes maps that locate the design high points and where to look for evidence of wear (the key to determining whether a coin exhibits circulation wear or meets the standards for Uncirculated). A digital version of this grading guide, with pinch zooming, is available free at iTunes for downloading on the iPad.

- *Official American Numismatic Association Grading Standards for United States Coins,* edited by Kenneth Bressett. This book features the ANA's official standards for grading U.S. coins accurately. Every standard grade is illustrated in high resolution and described in detail. Every coin is studied, from half cents to gold double eagles. Text descriptions of 30 levels help you pinpoint grades from Poor to perfect Mint State. All 11 levels of Mint State are discussed in detail, as are Proof designations.

- *Grading Coins by Photographs*, by Q. David Bowers—a combination of step-by-step grading instructions for every federal coinage series from half cents to double eagles, plus classic commemoratives. It also includes information on the history and importance of grading; expert grading techniques; understanding the surfaces of coins; and smart grading and buying. Bowers's insightful text is combined with enlarged high-resolution color photographs for each grade, plus Proofs. This book is spiralbound for easy handling.

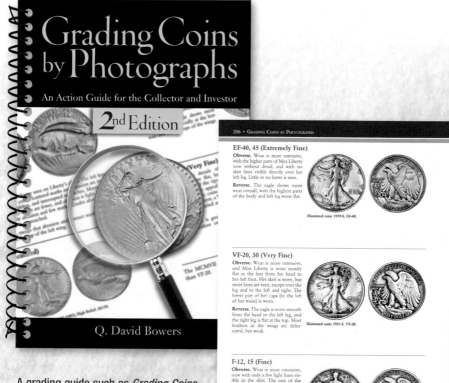

A grading guide such as *Grading Coins by Photographs* shows you, in pictures and words, how to analyze the condition of your coins.

- PCGS Photograde™ is an electronic-image coin grading guide available free (via iTunes) formatted for both the iPhone and iPad. It offers images of classic U.S. coins but does not provide images of modern circulating coins or bullion coins. No text (other than the grade) is provided. It offers pinch-zoom technology for enlarging the images.

ESSENTIAL TIPS FOR HANDLING COINS AND PAPER MONEY

Wash your hands. Before working with the coins, tokens, medals, or paper money, wash your hands with hot soapy water and dry them thoroughly.

Hold a coin, token, medal, or bank note by its edge. Whether using your bare hand or a glove, pick up the coin by its edge using your thumb and forefinger and continue to hold it between your thumb and forefinger while examining it. It is advisable to practice with larger-diameter coins such as dollars or half dollars in order to hone your skill before tackling smaller-diameter coins such as dimes and cents. Also, it may be helpful to practice using common coins from pocket change before attempting to pick up more valuable coins. Never pick up a coin so that your thumb or fingers cover the "heads" or "tails" side of the coin; this will leave fingerprints or acid and contaminants from your skin on the

The proper way to handle a coin is by the edge, between your thumb and forefinger—never touching the surfaces of the obverse and reverse.

surface of the coin. Use similar caution in picking up collectible paper money when the note is not in a clear plastic holder. Hold the paper money by its edges, taking care not to bend or crease it in any manner. If the note has a tear or holes in it, do not attempt to repair it or use tape of any kind.

When examining the coin, hold it over a coin pad or velvet cloth. Be sure to examine your coins in your planned, comfortable, and secure workspace with adequate lighting and keep them over the coin pad or velvet cloth.

Use velvet cloth as a resting place for the coin. If for any reason you need to temporarily place the coin on a surface before securing it in a holder, place it on the soft, velvet fabric surface.

Temporary storage. In addition to being secure, temporary storage for the coins and paper money you are working with should be in a cool, dry place, away from excessive heat and humidity. Especially for coins, if you are keeping them in your home, do not temporarily store them near the kitchen or where food is being prepared. Foods such as onions, egg yolks, and mayonnaise, when being cooked, release sulfur compounds that react with metals, especially silver. Also, cigarette smoke can be harmful to coins.

Paper money should also be handled with care.

Each part of a coin or piece of paper money has a name. Learn about each part, its location, and its role in imparting information you need to know.

3

THE BASICS OF IDENTIFICATION

Identifying your coins and other numismatic collectibles is a crucial step toward getting a fair offer when you go to sell them.

THE BASICS OF IDENTIFYING COINS

Before developing a list or creating an inventory of the coins that need to be identified, you need to be familiar with the important information a coin contains and know where to find it on the coin. The following information pertains to United States coins, but generally suffices for coins issued as money in most countries since the mid-16th century. Most of these terms are also applicable to tokens and medals.

A coin is usually made of metal and is authorized and issued by a government for use as money. A coin contains a design device authorized by the issuing government and usually states a monetary value, which is called its face value. Most coins are round, but they can be of different shapes and sizes. Many items, such as tokens, are coin-like and were used as money substitutes, but they are not coins because they were not issued by a government.

All coins have three sides: obverse, reverse, and edge.

obverse: Often referred to as the "heads" side, the obverse bears the dominant design or device, such as a portrait, as prescribed by the issuing authority. Often the obverse also bears a date.

reverse: Colloquially the reverse is dubbed the "tails" side. The reverse is the side opposite the obverse side. The reverse usually contains a specified design device that differs from the one on the obverse.

edge: Deemed the "third" side, the edge is the surface perpendicular to the obverse and reverse. Edges may be plain, lettered, or milled with repetitive devices such as reeds or emblems.

Coins also have parts which include design devices, an exergue, fields, and a rim.

device: The principal design element or symbol, such as a portrait, shield, or heraldic emblem on the obverse or reverse.

exergue: Pronounced "EX-urg." The area generally below the main design device. Often a date is in the exergue.

field: The flat area of the coin's surface surrounding and between the main design device, legends, or other design elements.

rim: The raised portion around the circumference of a coin.

Obverse.

Reverse.

Coins contain various types of information, which may be located on any of the three sides. However, such information is not always placed in the same location within the same denomination or on different coins of a particular design. The following terms are descriptive of the information:

date: Usually expressed in numerals, the date normally indicates the year of manufacture, which may or may not be the same as when the coin was issued, placed into circulation, or sold by the Mint. Sometimes coins carry multiple dates, especially those issued to commemorate a specific event or historical period.

denomination: The value stated on the coin. The denomination may be stated in words or numerals.

face value: The value stated on a coin. Face value is the minimum value of a particular monetary instrument and the amount for which it can be offered as legal tender.

legend: Words or a phrase that appear on a coin. Examples: LIBERTY and UNITED STATES OF AMERICA.

motto: A phrase or maxim. The United States has two official mottoes and both are required by law on U.S. coins: E PLURIBUS UNUM (Latin for "One Out of Many") and IN GOD WE TRUST.

mintmark: A letter or symbol denoting the facility in which the coin was produced. Mintmarks that appear on U.S. coins are:

C: Charlotte, North Carolina (gold coins only; 1838–1861)

CC: Carson City, Nevada (1870–1893)

D: Dahlonega, Georgia (gold coins only; 1838–1861)

D: Denver, Colorado (1906 to date)

O: New Orleans, Louisiana (1838–1861; 1879–1909)

P: Philadelphia, Pennsylvania (1793 to date; P not used in early years)

S: San Francisco, California (1854 to date)

W: West Point, New York (1984 to date)

designer/sculptor initials: One or more letters denoting the designer and/or sculptor who translated the coin design into a coin model. Sometimes one person created the design for both sides of the coin and rendered the coin model. However, especially in modern times, there may be two sets of initials on both the obverse and reverse, indicative of one artist creating the design and another sculpturing the model for one side of the coin. Different artists may have created the opposite side.

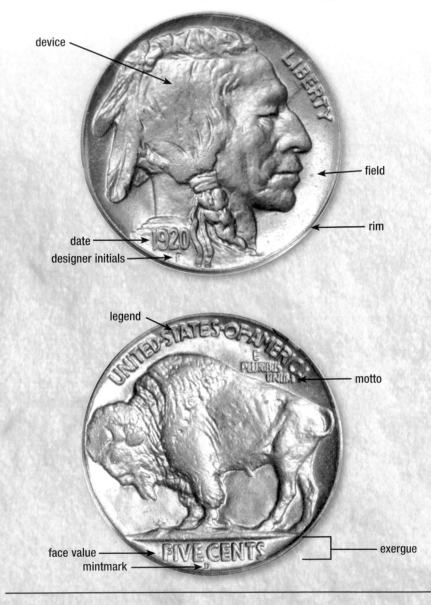

THE BASICS OF IDENTIFYING PAPER MONEY

The first paper money authorized by the United States government was issued in 1861. During the ensuing years, U.S. paper money has been issued in various types, denominations, sizes, and colors. Since our focus is to help identify what you may have, we will deal with basic terms that you will need to incorporate and list in your inventory.

As with coins, there is basic terminology specific to paper money.

face: The front side of a piece of paper money. The face is to paper money as the obverse is to a coin. In general, the face is the side with signatures and serial numbers.

back: The side opposite to the face of a piece of paper money. The back is to paper money as the reverse is to a coin.

Paper money contains design elements and information that are important to identification. While the various types of U.S. paper money contain different portraits, art elements, and various security devices, all contain some basic information.

denomination: The monetary value of a piece of paper money is expressed in numerals and text. On U.S. currency the numerals are usually located on the four corners of the note, on both the face and the back. The denomination is also expressed in words (for example, ONE DOLLAR) on both the front and back.

face value: The value stated on the piece of paper money. Face value is the minimum value of a particular monetary instrument and the amount for which it can be offered as legal tender.

signatures: Most federal U.S. currency produced since 1861 bears the signatures of at least two Treasury officials. In the early years, each note was hand-signed. In modern times the signatures are printed on the face side of the note.

serial number: Each note contains a unique serial number that may contain letters and numerals. The serial number is one of many security devices used on paper money. It appears twice on each note and is exactly the same in each place.

series number: The series number does not necessarily indicate the calendar year in which the note was printed. A series begins with the year it was introduced. Series change when a new design is introduced or designating the first year of the term of a new secretary of the Treasury and a new treasurer. If the treasurer changes during the secretary's tenure, a suffix letter is added to the year, which is retained.

Face.

Back.

type: Generally at the top of the face side, the type of note is identified. Some examples: Federal Reserve Note, Federal Reserve Bank Note, Silver Certificate, Gold Certificate, Legal Tender Note, National Bank Note.

vignette: Most paper currency contains a portrait or art element, generally on the face. For example, the $1 bill bears a portrait vignette of George Washington. Generally the person is identified by last name below the portrait.

vignette

denomination

serial number

series number

signatures

Gain an understanding of the scope of your collection or accumulation of coins with tips on sorting, first by the color of the metal and then by denomination.

4

THE ADVENTURE BEGINS

I t is possible that you have no idea as to what coins or other numismatic items are in the collection and they are in a bank vault or safety deposit box. In such cases it may be wise to plan an initial visit and ask the bank official in charge of the vault or safety deposit box if there is a private room (without windows) in the bank that could be available to you for several hours where you could initially examine the contents. Remember to take your velvet cloth, magnifier, and gloves if you have decided to use them.

SORTING

Whether working in a bank vault or within a secure location in your home, one of the first tasks you face is to begin to understand the scope of the collection or accumulation. If you are attempting to identify more than 100 coins, it is advisable to sort the coins first by metallic composition and then by denomination. Sorting will help in two ways: It will provide an initial understanding of the size of the collection or accumulation, and it will provide a basic structure for organizing your work and estimating the time you may need to identify and inventory the coins.

It is likely that all or most of the coins in your collection or accumulation are United States coins. If you encounter coins (or pieces of paper money) that do not have UNITED STATES OF AMERICA on them, they were not manufactured in the United States. (U.S. *medals* and *tokens*, however, do not necessarily have the name of the country on them. See chapter 8.) In the initial sorting, set aside any non-U.S. items. Chapter 8 provides information and resources for identifying foreign coins and non-U.S. paper money.

Initial Sort: Color

The first sort should be by color and metal composition.

U.S. coins are one of three basic colors: brown, white, or yellow. The basic colors stem from the fact that U.S. coins struck from 1792 through 1964 are primarily made of copper, silver, or gold. The exceptions are coins made with nickel, which have a silver-like appearance, and steel cents made during World War II. Since 1997, the U.S. Mint has struck platinum bullion coins. In 2000 the Mint began to issue dollar coins made of a new alloy: manganese-brass. Although golden in color when new, manganese-brass coins contain no gold and they tarnish to brown when extensively circulated.

Copper coins include half cents and large cents (1790s to 1850s), small cents (1850s to date), and two-cent pieces (1860s and 1870s).

Copper coins. When copper coins are first struck, they are bright orange. However, copper quickly reacts with oxygen and begins to turn brown. Copper coins also react to the oil and acid in human skin, so as copper coins pass from hand to hand in circulation, the brown coloring accelerates.

Silver coins. Silver is free of color and white in appearance. However, it reacts with elements such as oxygen and sulfur. Depending on the degree of circulation and their exposure to the environment, silver coins may tarnish, exhibiting a range of colors from light yellow to a dark greyish black.

Nickel (copper-nickel) coins. Often nickel-alloy coins are mistaken for silver coins because nickel is also "white" in appearance. However, nickel does not tarnish as quickly as silver. Modern dimes (post-1964), quarters (post-1964), and half dollars (post-1970) have a copper core layered with an alloy of copper-nickel. Five-cent pieces are coined in an alloy of copper-nickel.

Silver coins generally date from the 1960s and earlier, although some modern coins are struck in silver for collectors.

Nickel has been used in U.S. coins, in various alloys, since the 1860s.

Steel coins. In 1943, in order to conserve copper as a strategic war material, the U.S. Mint made one-cent coin of steel coated in zinc. This coinage composition tarnished easily over time, so many 1943 cents today are seen with spots of rust.

Platinum coins. Platinum to the untrained eye looks like silver because it is also "white" in appearance. However, platinum is more brittle than silver and is a rarer metal. Platinum has never been used for circulation-strike coins in the United States. Platinum bullion coins (American Platinum Eagles) are identified as platinum on the coin.

The U.S. Mint saved millions of pounds of copper by switching to a *steel* cent during World War II.

In the United States, platinum has never been used in pocket-change coins. Today the precious metal is available as a bullion product from the U.S. Mint.

Gold coins. Called the "yellow" metal, gold ranges in color from a light yellow to a deep orange-gold. Because pure gold is relatively soft, it is alloyed with silver and copper to make it more sturdy and coinable. Silver-alloyed gold coins are soft yellow in color, whereas the addition of copper tips the color scale toward the deeper orange-gold hues.

Manganese-brass coins. An alloy that is golden in color, manganese-brass turns brown when exposed to oxygen over time and when subjected to skin oils and acid.

U.S. gold coins range from tiny gold dollars (smaller than a dime) to massive $50 "slugs."

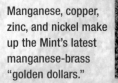

Manganese, copper, zinc, and nickel make up the Mint's latest manganese-brass "golden dollars."

Second Sort: Denomination

After sorting by color/metal composition, the next logical step is to sort by denomination.

Circulation coins (struck for use in commerce). The denominations of U.S. coins struck for circulation are metal-specific:

> *Copper and bronze alloys*—half cent, one-cent, two-cents.
>
> *Silver*—Prior to 1965: three-cents, five-cents of 1943–1945, half dime, dime, twenty-cents, quarter dollar, half dollar (also struck in a 40% silver alloy from 1965 to 1970), dollar.
>
> *Copper-nickel*—three-cents, five-cents; since 1965: dime, quarter, dollar; since 1971: half dollar.
>
> *Steel*—one-cent of 1943.
>
> *Gold*—$1, $2.50, $3, $5, $10, $20, $25, $50.
>
> *Platinum*—$10, $25, $50, $100.
>
> *Manganese-brass*—Since 2000: $1.

U.S. commemorative coins. Struck to honor a person, place, or event, commemorative coins have generally been issued in either silver or gold. Because they normally are sold to collectors for a premium and have low mintages compared to circulation-strike coins, they usually do not circulate. However, a few silver commemoratives in the early series (1892

The United States released hundreds of different commemorative coins since 1892.

to 1954) were sold at face value and made their way into circulation. Because they were "different," the general public tended to save the silver commemorative coins when they were found in pocket change.

Classic commemorative series, 1892 to 1954—Most early commemoratives are silver half dollars, although there also are quarter and dollar silver commemoratives. Gold denominations in the classic series include $1, $2.50, and $50.

Modern commemorative series, 1982 to date—The silver dollar is the most prevalent denomination, although there are some silver half dollar commemoratives. Copper-nickel alloy (often referred to as "clad") has been used for some modern half dollar commemoratives. The $5 denomination dominates in the modern gold commemoratives. There are a few $10 gold commemoratives.

U.S. bullion coins. The U.S. Mint began producing silver and gold bullion coins in 1986. Platinum bullion coins were added in 1997. A bullion coin is valued by the market price of the precious metal contained within it, plus overhead including manufacturing costs. Each coin states its precious-metal content and the weight in troy ounces. U.S. bullion coins are denominated and are legal tender for their face value, although in practicality selling a bullion coin for its face value would result in a significant loss. Denominations of U.S. bullion coins include:

U.S. bullion coins are issued individually, in bulk lots, and in special sets (like this 1993 Philadelphia Mint Bicentennial set, with a commemorative medal).

Silver—quarter dollar (five-ounce America the Beautiful series); $1

Gold—$5, $10, $25, $50

Platinum—$10, $25, $50, $100

PRACTICAL CONSIDERATIONS

If most of the coins you find are made of precious metals—gold, silver, or platinum—and have been stored in bank vaults or in safety deposit boxes, it would be wise to leave them in the secure environment until you complete the inventory. In such cases, it would be advisable to make arrangements for use of a private room within the storage facility for your inventory work. Likewise, if you find significant quantities of coins made of silver, gold, or platinum stored at the person's home or other locations, it would be prudent to locate secure storage for the coins on a temporary basis.

Typically accumulations and casual collections have been kept at the home of the person who saved or collected the coins. They may have been stored in a home safe or in boxes or other containers in various parts of the house. The coins may be in coin folders, coin albums, coin boards, coin flips, 2-by-2 holders, special sonically sealed coin holders, or small envelopes, or wrapped in paper rolls or original packaging from the issuing mint. Or they may be loose in buckets, jars, shoeboxes, or other containers.

Once you have sorted the coins by metal compositions and denominations, you should begin to have an idea of the quantity of coins you are dealing with. You can plan blocks of time to further identify them and prepare the inventory. This will lead you to your first practical decision: Is it worth my time and effort to inventory every coin?

Many accumulations and casual collections contain hundreds or possibly thousands of coins of the same denomination. Most often these "mini hoards" are comprised of Lincoln cents, the longest continuously produced (1909 to date) U.S. design series for a denomination; or of silver dimes, quarters, and half dollars dated prior to 1965. Silver coins dated before 1965 are made of 90 percent silver, and half dollars of 1965 to 1970 are 40 percent silver, so they have a bullion value and may have a collector premium as well.

Lincoln cents are a different story. While there may be key dates and varieties that have significant collector value mixed in the "piles," you will have to weigh your time versus likely reward. Ascertaining when the coins may have been saved or collected gives you useful information. The most valuable Lincoln cents are those bearing the Wheat reverse, dated 1909 through 1958. If you do not know the period of time during which the coins were acquired, take some random samples. If you find that most have the Wheat reverse, it may pay to sort by date and mint-mark. If Memorial reverse cents (1959 to 2008) are mixed in or consti-tute the majority, it still may be worth the time and effort to locate the Wheat reverses and set them aside.

The Wheat reverse coins are 95 percent copper, with an average weight of 3.11 grams each. (There is a one-year exception. Lincoln cents produced in 1943 are made of zinc-coated steel, are grey in color, and weigh from 2.69 grams to 2.75 grams each.)

Wheat cents are commonly found in accumulations—filling rolls, bags, boxes, jars, and other containers.

Since the vast majority of Wheat reverse cents are made of 95 percent copper, it is best to use the 3.11 grams for average weight. We know that 1 pound is equal to 453.592 grams. Thus, if we divide 453.592 by 3.11, we find that there are 145.849 one-cent coins in a pound. Round that to 146 to simplify your math calculations.

Weigh your cache of "Wheaties." (If they are in a container, first weigh them in the container and record the total weight. Then take the coins out of the container and weigh the container. The total weight minus the weight of the container will give you the weight of the coins.)

As an example, let's assume you have 95 pounds of Lincoln, Wheat reverse cents. As this book was being finalized in April 2014, coin dealers and Lincoln cent specialists were offering an average of 2 to 3 cents per coin for bags of "unsearched" Wheat cents, or $2.92 to $4.38 per pound. So for 95 pounds a reasonable offer would range from $277.10 to $461.10. If you decide to sell the coins in bulk or by the pound, it is best to find a local buyer or make arrangements to sell your coins to a collector or dealer nearby. Shipping costs for 95 pounds of coins plus the container could quickly eat up your profit.

All U.S. coins, regardless of when they were produced by the Mint, are still worth their face value if you take them to your local bank. Your 95 pounds of Wheat reverse cents would likely contain 13,855 one-cent coins, so the 95 pounds are worth a minimum of $138.55.

Sorting your 95 pounds of coins by date and mintmark could be rewarding because some of the most valuable Lincoln cents were produced between 1909 and 1958. One example: During the first year of issue, some cents struck at the San Francisco Mint bear the designer's initials, V.D.B. (for Victor David Brenner), on the reverse. Retail values in April 2014 for a 1909-S V.D.B. ranged from $650 for a heavily worn specimen to more than $100,000 for an example graded MS-67 Red. Another example: One of the most famous of the error coins in the Lincoln series dates from 1955. It is called a *doubled die* by collectors. Each numeral in the date on the obverse literally has two numerals for each digit; this can be easily seen without the aid of a magnifying glass. Retail values in 2014 for the 1955 Doubled Die Obverse ranged from $2,200 for a coin with moderate wear to more than $40,000 for one graded MS-65 Red. Of course, not all of the dates and mintmarks carry collector values as high as this, but many of Lincoln cents produced between 1909 and 1925 retail for several dollars each, even in the lower grades.

If you have the time and resources—primarily in human terms—sorting Wheat cents by date and mintmark can be fun and profitable. It is an excellent family activity, especially for children between the ages of 9 and 12, if they have a supervising adult overseeing the project. One economical method is to obtain several packages of paper or foam cups that can be marked. You will need one cup for each date and mintmark plus some for the major varieties collected in the series, which numbers approximately 160. (Check your price guide or check list for the dates and mintmarks.) You will also need a number of tables or lots of counter space on which to place the cups. Provide each person sorting with a bag or bucket of coins and invite them to place the coins in the appropriate cups. Since some dates and mintmarks were produced in greater numbers and have survived in greater numbers, the cups will contain varying numbers of coins when the sorting is completed. The quantities will likely follow the value ratings, with the more valuable coins being fewer in number. Once sorted, you are ready to record the results in the inventory.

Sorting by date and mintmark is recommended for any large group of coins. Chapter 5 will be of help as you sort U.S. coins by design type; Chapter 7 will help in a similar way as you identify and sort U.S. paper money by type.

The famous 1955 Doubled Die Obverse variety is just one of many valuable coins in the Wheat cent series. Searching through an accumulation can be worth your time if you find one. (shown enlarged)

Here's a quick identifier for each U.S. coin struck for circulation from 1792 to date, by design type, with enlarged and actual-size photos to assist you.

5

IDENTIFYING COINS BY DESIGN TYPE

N ow that you have sorted your coins by color and denomination, you are ready to identify them by design type. This chapter displays U.S. coins by type struck for circulation from 1792 to date as well as a section for bullion coins produced since 1986. (U.S. commemorative coins also are listed and pictured in this chapter.) The chapter is organized by metallic content, meaning that all copper coins struck for circulation are listed in a color-keyed section, progressing from the lowest denomination to the highest. Likewise, color-keyed sections for nickel, silver, gold, and manganese-brass are also provided and each progresses from the lowest denomination to the highest. Metallic composition changes are noted, but the design type is not repeated. For example, Washington quarters from 1932 through 1964 were 90 percent silver and 10 percent copper. Since 1965 they have been produced of a pure copper core with outer layers of copper-nickel (75 percent copper and 25 percent nickel). The metallic changes are noted, but the Washington quarter is not listed in the nickel or copper-nickel section. The bullion section is organized in a similar manner—silver, gold, and platinum—from the lowest to highest denomination for each metal.

It is possible to use a price guide that has actual-size images of the coins to identify design types. However, this chapter is designed as a quick reference guide. It is organized by color/metallic content, denomination, and design type.

top of the page: Identifies the design type, denomination, and years of issue.

enlarged images: Obverse and reverse images help to identify the design type.

actual-size images: A second illustration of the coin's obverse is the same size as the actual coin. The diameter of the coin is provided in millimeters and inches. (This is useful information because replicas of U.S. coins are commonly encountered and often they are of a different size than the real coin.)

obverse design: Description of the design and the designer's name.

reverse design: Description of the design and the designer's name. If multiple reverse design have been used within the issue, descriptions of additional designs and dates of issue are included.

edge: Description of the coin's edge.

mintmarks: Letters for each of the production facilities that struck the design and denomination.

metallic content: Alloy content. Dates of issue are included, if alloy changes were made. (This is important because replicas and counterfeits often do not use the same alloy as the real coin.)

weight: Stated in both grams and avoirdupois ounces for copper and nickel; grams and troy ounces for silver, gold, and platinum.

location of mintmark: Written description of location of the mintmark on the coin.

important dates: The most valuable dates and mintmark combinations in the design series.

notes: Other important information that you should be aware of when examining coins of this design and denomination.

OVERVIEW OF U.S. COIN DESIGNS

Following the dictates of the Mint Act of 1792, U.S. coins for the nation's first two centuries carried an obverse design emblematic of liberty, which was most often depicted as an allegorical representation in a female persona. The law also specified that the inscription LIBERTY and the year the coin was struck were to be on the obverse. On the reverse, the law directed that silver and gold coins were to depict an eagle and carry the inscription UNITED STATES OF AMERICA. Copper coins were to have an inscription stating the denomination on the reverse. The first departure from these design dictates for circulating coins occurred in 1909 when Abraham Lincoln's portrait was placed on the one-cent denomination. Within 62 years a transition to presidential portraits on the obverses had transpired: Washington on the quarter in 1932, Jefferson on the five-cent piece in 1938, Franklin D. Roosevelt on the dime in 1946, John F. Kennedy on the half dollar in 1964, and Dwight D. Eisenhower on the dollar in 1971. The change to the small-sized dollar coin in 1979 offered an opportunity to depart the presidential cycle. Suffragist Susan B. Anthony was selected, but because the coin was too often confused with the quarter dollar, it failed to circulate widely. An attempt to revive the small-dollar coin brought Sacagawea's portrait to the denomination in 2000. It, too, failed to circulate widely. Presidents returned to the dollar coin in 2007, with four new portraits each year through mid-2016. At least 38 presidents will be honored on the small-dollar coin. The authorizing law prohibits a living president being depicted.

Location of Mintmark

From 1792 to 1837 it was unnecessary to place a mintmark on a U.S. coin because all were produced at the Philadelphia Mint. With the opening of branch mints in 1838 in Charlotte (North Carolina), Dahlonega (Georgia), and New Orleans (Louisiana), letters were placed on the coins to identify where they had been struck. As additional mint-ing facilities opened, the practice continued. They include:

C—Charlotte, North Carolina (gold coins only; 1838–1861)
CC—Carson City, Nevada (1870–1893)
D—Dahlonega, Georgia (gold coins only; 1838–1861)
D—Denver, Colorado (1906 to date)
O—New Orleans, Louisiana (1838–1861; 1879–1909)
P—Philadelphia, Pennsylvania (1793 to date; P not used in early years)
S—San Francisco, California (1854 to date)
W—West Point, New York (1984 to date)

Often referred to as the Mother Mint, the Philadelphia Mint has struck coins continuously since its opening in 1792, except for a brief closure in 1814 due to an epidemic of yellow fever. However, the P mintmark did not become a mainstay on most denominations until the mid-1900s and later.

The first use of the P mintmark was from 1942 to 1945 on Jefferson five-cent coins. Mintmarks were used on the silver-alloy five-cent coins during this four-year period so they could be distinguished easily from the traditional copper-nickel alloy. The U.S. Mint began using the P mintmark on the new, small-sized Anthony dollar in 1979, and then in 1980 began using it on all coins (except the Lincoln cent) struck at the Philadelphia facility. That practice continues.

There are a couple of exceptions to these guidelines regarding mint-marks. Due to a nationwide coin shortage and to discourage hoarding, the U.S. Mint suspended the practice of using mintmarks on all U.S. coins struck for circulation dated 1965 through 1967. Also, during the 1970s and 1980s the Mint did not place mintmarks on coins (primarily cents) produced at San Francisco and West Point, which were at the time designated assay offices rather than mints.

COPPER U.S. COINS
LIBERTY CAP HALF CENT (1793–1797)

Actual size:
22 mm / 0.87 in.

Actual size:
22 mm / 0.87 in.

Obverses: (1793) Liberty Cap, Head Facing Left, probably designed by Joseph Wright, engraved by Henry Voigt. (1794–1797) Liberty Cap, Head Facing Right: 1794 possibly designed by Joseph Wright, engraved by Robert Scot; 1795 large head by John Smith Gardner; 1795–1797 small head by Gardner.
Reverse: Laurel wreath by Joseph Wright.
Edges: (1793) Lettered TWO HUNDRED FOR A DOLLAR.

(1794–1795) Lettered TWO HUNDRED FOR A DOLLAR. (1795–1796) Plain. (1797) Some lettered and some plain.
Mintmark: None (all struck at the Philadelphia Mint).
Metallic content: 100 percent copper.
Weights: (1793) 6.74 grams / 0.23 oz. (1794–1795) 6.74 grams / 0.23 oz. (1795–1797) 5.44 grams / 0.19 oz.
Important dates: All 1793 issues are scarce; the key date of the series is 1796.

DRAPED BUST HALF CENT (1800–1808)

Actual size:
23.5 mm / 0.93 in.

Obverse: Draped bust of Liberty by Gilbert Stuart, translated to coin model by John Eckstein; engraved by Robert Scot.
Reverse: Laurel wreath by Joseph Wright, engraved by Robert Scot and John Smith Gardner.
Edge: Plain.

Mintmark: None (all struck at the Philadelphia Mint).
Metallic content: 100 percent copper.
Weight: 5.44 grams / 0.19 oz.
Important dates: 1802; 1806, Small 5, With Stems.

CLASSIC HEAD HALF CENT (1809–1836)

Actual size:
23.5 mm / 0.93 in.

Obverse: Head of Liberty facing left, wearing LIBERTY headband, by John Reich.
Reverse: Continuous laurel wreath, by John Reich.
Edge: Plain.

Mintmark: None (all struck at the Philadelphia Mint).
Metallic content: 100 percent copper.
Weight: 5.44 grams / 0.19 oz.
Important date: 1811.

BRAIDED HAIR HALF CENT (1840–1857)

Actual size:
23.5 mm / 0.93 in.

Obverse: Liberty facing left wearing a coronet, by Christian Gobrecht.
Reverse: Continuous wreath based on John Reich's design.
Edge: Plain.

Mintmark: None (all struck at the Philadelphia Mint).
Metallic content: 100 percent copper.
Weight: 5.44 grams / 0.19 oz.
Important date: 1849, Large Date.

FLOWING HAIR CENT (1793)

Actual size:
26–27 mm / ~1.02 in.

Actual size:
26–28 mm / ~1.02 in.

Obverse: Liberty with flowing hair, by Robert Birch.
Reverses: Chain reverse by Birch; Wreath reverse by Birch.
Edges: Vine and bar, or lettered ONE HUNDRED FOR A DOLLAR.

Mintmark: None (all struck at the Philadelphia Mint).
Metallic content: 100% copper.
Weight: 13.48 grams / 0.47 oz.
Important dates: All varieties are rare; the key is the Wreath, Strawberry Leaf variety.

LIBERTY CAP CENT (1793–1796)

Actual size: 28.5 mm / 1.13 in.

Obverse: Liberty Cap, by Joseph Wright.
Reverse: Wreath, by Joseph Wright.
Edges: Plain, or lettered ONE HUNDRED FOR A DOLLAR.
Mintmark: None (all struck at the Philadelphia Mint).

Metallic content: 100% copper.
Weights: (1793–1795) 13.4 grams / 0.47 oz. (1795–1796) 10.89 grams / 0.38 oz.
Important dates: 1793; 1794, Starred Reverse; 1795, Jefferson Head, Plain Edge (not a regular Mint issue).

DRAPED BUST CENT (1796–1807)

Actual size:
28.5 mm / 1.13 in.

Obverse: Draped Bust, by Gilbert Stuart / John Eckstein.
Reverse: Wreath, by Joseph Wright.
Edge: Plain.
Mintmark: None (all struck at the Philadelphia Mint).

Metallic content: 100% copper.
Weight: 10.89 grams / 0.38 oz.
Important dates: 1799; 1799, 9 Over 8; 1803, Large Date, Small Fraction; 1807, 7 Over 6, Small 7.

CLASSIC HEAD CENT (1808–1814)

Actual size:
28.5 mm / 1.13 in.

Obverse: Classic Head, by John Reich.
Reverse: Laurel Wreath, by John Reich.
Edge: Plain.
Mintmark: None (all struck at the Philadelphia Mint).

Metallic content: 100% copper.
Weight: 10.89 grams / 0.38 oz.
Important dates: 1809; 1811; 1811, Last 1 Over 0.

LIBERTY HEAD CENT (1816–1857)

Actual size:
28.5 mm / 1.13 in.

Obverses: (1816–1835) Matron Head, by Robert Scot. (1835–1839) Matron Head modified ("Young Head"), by Robert Scot and Christian Gobrecht. (1839–1857) Braided Hair, by Scot and Gobrecht.
Reverses: (1816–1839) Laurel Wreath, by John Reich. (1839–1857) Laurel Wreath, by Reich/Gobrecht.

Edge: Plain.
Mintmark: None (all struck at the Philadelphia Mint).
Metallic content: 100% copper.
Weight: 10.89 grams / 0.38 oz.
Important dates: 1823; 1823, 3 Over 2; 1834, Large 8, Large Stars, Medium Letters; 1839, 9 Over 6.

FLYING EAGLE CENT (1856–1858)

Actual size:
19.3 mm / 0.76 in.

Obverse: Flying Eagle, by Christian Gobrecht and James B. Longacre.
Reverse: Agricultural Wreath, by James B. Longacre.
Edge: Plain.

Mintmark: None (all struck at the Philadelphia Mint).
Metallic content: 88% copper, 12% nickel.
Weight: 4.67 grams / 0.16 oz.
Important date: 1856.

INDIAN HEAD CENT (1859–1909)

Actual size:
(1859–1864)
19.3 mm / 0.76 in.
(1864–1909)
19.05 mm / 0.75 in.

Obverse: Indian Head (Liberty in a war bonnet), by James B. Longacre.
Reverse: Agricultural Wreath, by James B. Longacre.
Edge: Plain.
Mintmark: No mintmark for those struck at the Philadelphia Mint. S mintmark, located under the wreath, for 1908 and 1909 coins struck at the San Francisco Mint.

Metallic content: (1859–1864) 88% copper, 12% nickel. (1864–1909) 95% copper, 5% tin and zinc.
Weights: (1859–1864) 4.67 grams / 0.16 oz. (1864–1909) 3.11 grams / 0.11 oz.
Important dates: 1877; 1888, 8 Over 7; 1909-S.

LINCOLN CENT (1909 TO DATE)

Actual size:
19 mm / 0.75 in.

1909–1958, Wheat Ears reverse.

1959–2008, Memorial reverse.

2009, Birth and Early Childhood reverse.

2009, Formative Years reverse.

2009, Professional Life reverse.

2009, Presidency reverse.

2010 to date, Shield reverse.

Obverse: Abraham Lincoln portrait, by David Victor Brenner.
Reverses: (1909–1958) Wheat Ears, by David Victor Brenner. (1959–2008) Lincoln Memorial, by Frank Gasparro. (2009) Bicentennial: Kentucky, log cabin; Indiana, rail-splitter; Illinois, Capitol; District of Columbia, U.S. Capitol. (2010 to date) Union Shield, by Lyndall Bass.
Edge: Plain.
Mintmarks: D and S; Philadelphia Mint cents do not have a mintmark.
Metallic content: (1909–1942) 95% copper, 5% tin and zinc. (1942) 95% copper, 5% zinc. (1943) Zinc-coated steel. (1944–1946) 95% copper, 5% zinc. (1947–1962) 95% copper, 5% tin and zinc. (1962–1982) 95% copper, 5% zinc. (1982 to date) 97.5% zinc, 2.5% copper (except 2009 collector versions, 95% copper, 3% zinc, 2% tin).
Weights: (1909–1942) 3.11 grams. (1943) 2.70 grams. (1944–1982) 3.11 grams. (1982 to date) 2.50 grams.
Designer's initials: Brenner's initials (V.D.B.) appear at the bottom-center reverse, next to the rim, only in 1909. His initials were placed on the obverse at the bottom of Lincoln's shoulder, next to the rim, beginning in 1918.
Important dates: 1909-S V.D.B.; 1909-S; 1914-D; 1922, No D; 1943, bronze; 1943-D, bronze; 1943-S, bronze; 1955, Doubled Die Obverse; 1969-S, Doubled Die Obverse; 1970-S, Doubled Die Obverse; 1972, Doubled Die Obverse; 1984, Doubled Die Obverse; 1990, No S (Proof); 1995, Doubled Die Obverse.

SHIELD TWO-CENT PIECE (1864–1872)

Actual size:
23 mm / 0.91 in.

Obverse: Shield, by James B. Longacre.

Reverse: Agricultural wreath, with 2 CENTS in center, by James B. Longacre.

Edge: Plain.

Mintmark: None (all struck at the Philadelphia Mint).

Metallic content: 95% copper, 5% tin and zinc.

Weight: 6.22 grams / 0.22 oz.

Important dates: 1864 Small Motto; 1867, Double Die Obverse; 1872; 1873, Closed 3, Proof; 1873, Open 3, Proof restrike.

NICKEL U.S.COINS
(Copper-Nickel Alloy)
NICKEL THREE-CENT PIECES (1865–1889)

Actual size:
17.9 mm / 0.71 in.

Obverse: Head of Liberty, by James B. Longacre.

Reverse: Laurel wreath with Roman numeral III in the center, by James B. Longacre.

Edge: Plain.

Mintmark: None (all struck at the Philadelphia Mint).

Metallic content: 75% copper, 25% nickel.

Weight: 1.94 grams / 0.06 oz.

Important dates: 1882; 1883; 1884; 1885; 1887; Proofs struck in 1877, 1878, 1886, and 1887, 7 Over 6.

NICKEL

SHIELD NICKEL (1866–1883)

Actual size:
20.5 mm / 0.81 in.

Obverse: Shield by James B. Longacre.
Reverses: (1866–1867) 13 stars with rays, numeral 5 in center, by James B. Longacre. (1867–1883) 13 stars without rays, numeral 5 in center, by Longacre.
Edge: Plain.
Mintmark: None (all struck at the Philadelphia Mint).

Metallic content: 75% copper, 25% nickel.
Weight: 5 grams / 0.17 oz.
Important dates: 1866, Repunched Date; 1871; 1879; 1880; 1881; 1883, 3 Over 2; Proofs struck in 1877, 1878, and 1879, 9 Over 8.

LIBERTY HEAD NICKEL (1883–1912)

Actual size:
21.21 mm / 0.84 in.

Obverse: Liberty Head, by Charles Barber.
Reverses: (1883) Harvest wreath, Roman numeral V in center, without CENTS legend, by Charles Barber. (1883–1912) Same, but with CENTS below the wreath.
Edge: Plain.
Mintmarks: No mintmark for coins struck at the Philadelphia

Mint; mintmarks only in 1912 (D and S, on reverse, to the left of CENTS).
Metallic content: 75% copper, 25% nickel
Weight: 5 grams / 0.17 oz.
Important dates: 1885; 1886; 1912-S; Proof 1913.

INDIAN HEAD (BUFFALO) NICKEL (1913–1938)

Actual size:
21.21 mm / 0.84 in.

Obverse: Indian Head, by James Earle Fraser.

Reverses: (1913) American Bison standing on a mound, by James Earle Fraser. (1913–1938) Bison standing on a plain, by James Earle Fraser.

Edge: Plain.

Mintmarks: No mintmark for coins struck at the Philadelphia Mint; D and S on the reverse, below FIVE CENTS.

Metallic content: 75% copper, 25% nickel.

Weight: 5 grams / 0.17 oz.

Important dates: 1913-S; 1914, 4 Over 3; 1916, Doubled Die Obverse; 1918-D, 8 Over 7; 1936-D, 3-1/2 Legs; 1937-D, 3-Legged.

JEFFERSON NICKEL (1938 TO DATE)

Actual size:
21.21 mm / 0.84 in.

2004 obverse.   2004, Peace Medal reverse.   2004, Keelboat reverse.

| 2005 obverse. | 2005, American Bison reverse. | 2005, Ocean in View reverse. | 2006 to date obverse. | 2006 to date reverse. |

Obverses: (1938–2004) Thomas Jefferson portrait, by Felix Schlag. (2005) Thomas Jefferson portrait, by Joe Fitzgerald. (2006) Thomas Jefferson portrait, by Jamie Franki.

Reverses: (1938–2003) Monticello, by Felix Schlag. (2004) Peace Medal, by Norman E. Nemeth; Keelboat, by Al Maletsky. (2005) American Bison, by Jamie Franki; Ocean in View, by Joe Fitzgerald. (2006 to date) Monticello, by Felix Schlag.

Edge: Plain.

Mintmarks: (1938–1942, 1946–1964) D and S on the reverse, to the right of Monticello. (1942–1945) P, D, or S on the reverse, above the dome of Monticello.

(1968–2004) D or S on the obverse, below and to the right of Jefferson's queue (ponytail). (2005) D or S below LIBERTY on the obverse. (2006 to date) D or S below the date, on the obverse.

Metallic content: (1938–1942) 75% copper, 25% nickel. (1942–1945) 56% copper, 35% silver, 9% manganese. (1946 to date) 75% copper, 25% nickel.

Weight: (copper-nickel) 5 grams / 0.17 oz.

Actual silver weight: (1942–1945) 1.75 grams / 0.05626 oz.

Important dates: 1939, Doubled MONTICELLO; 1942-D, D Over Horizontal D; Proof 1971-S, No S; 1997-P, Matte Finish.

ANTHONY DOLLAR (1979–1981, 1999)

Actual size: 26.5 mm / 1.05 in.

Obverse: Portrait of Susan B. Anthony, by Frank Gasparro.
Reverse: Eagle landing on the moon, by Frank Gasparro.
Edge: Reeded.
Mintmarks: P, D, S, on the obverse, on the left, above Anthony's shoulder.

Metallic content: 75% copper, 25% nickel bonded to a pure copper core.
Weight: 8.1 grams / 0.28 oz.
Important dates: 1979-P, Near Date, Wide Rim.
Note: Grade rarity is a factor in grades MS-65 and up for all dates.

MANGANESE-BRASS U.S. COINS
SACAGAWEA DOLLAR (2000–2008)

Actual size:
26.5 mm / 1.05 in.

Obverse: Sacagawea carrying her infant son on her back, by Glenna Goodacre.
Reverse: Eagle in flight, with 17 stars surrounding, by Thomas G. Rogers Sr.
Edge: Plain.
Mintmarks: P, D, S, on the obverse, below the date.

Metallic content: Outer layer of 77% copper, 12% zinc, 7% manganese, and 4% nickel, bonded to a pure copper core.
Weight: 8.1 grams / 0.28 oz.
Important dates: 2000-P, Cheerios Reverse; 2000-P, Goodacre Presentation Finish.
Note: Grade rarity is a factor in grades MS-68 and above.

MANGANESE-BRASS

NATIVE AMERICAN DOLLAR (2009 TO DATE)

Actual size:
26.5 mm / 1.05 in.

2009, Three
Sisters reverse.

2010, Great Law
of Peace reverse.

2011, Wampanoag
Treaty reverse.

2012, Trade Routes in the
17th Century reverse.

2013, Treaty With the
Delawares reverse.

2014, Native
Hospitality reverse.

Obverse: Modified Sacagawea carrying her infant son on her back, by Glenna Goodacre.

Reverses: New reverse each year honoring Native Americans through at least 2016. (2009) Three Sisters. (2010) Great Law of Peace. (2011) Wampanoag Treaty. (2012) Trade Routes in the 17th Century. (2013) Treaty With the Delawares. (2014) Native Hospitality Ensured the Success of the Lewis and Clark Expedition.

Edge: Date, mintmark, three stars, E PLURIBUS UNUM, 10 stars.

Mintmarks: P, D, S, on the edge.

Metallic content: Outer layer of 77% copper, 12% zinc, 7% manganese, and 4% nickel, bonded to a pure copper core.

Weight: 8.1 grams / 0.28 oz.

Important date: 2009-P, Three Sisters.

Note: Grade rarity is a factor in grades MS-68 and above.

PRESIDENTIAL DOLLAR (2007 TO DATE)

Actual size:
26.5 mm / 1.05 in.

Date, mintmark,
and mottos
incused on edge.

See the following pages for illustrations of all Presidential dollars issued to date.

Obverses: Portraits of presidents of the United States, by various designers, issued at the rate of four per year (through at least 2016) in the presidents' order of service. The motto IN GOD WE TRUST was moved from the edge to the obverse in 2009. (2007) Washington, John Adams, Jefferson, Madison. (2008) Monroe, John Quincy Adams, Jackson, Van Buren. (2009) William Henry Harrison, Tyler, Polk, Taylor. (2010) Fillmore, Pierce, Buchanan, Lincoln. (2011) Andrew Johnson, Grant, Hayes, Garfield. (2012) Arthur, Cleveland [first administration], Benjamin Harrison, Cleveland [second administration]. (2013) McKinley, Theodore Roosevelt, Taft, Wilson. (2014) Harding, Coolidge, Hoover, Franklin D. Roosevelt. (2015) Truman, Eisenhower, Kennedy, Lyndon Johnson. (2016) Nixon, Ford.

Reverse: Statue of Liberty, by Donald C. Everhart II.

Edges: (2007–2008) Date, mintmark, E PLURIBUS UNUM, dot, IN GOD WE TRUST, dot. (2009 to date) Date, mintmark, three stars, E PLURIBUS UNUM, 10 stars.

Mintmarks: P, D, S, on the edge.

Metallic content: Outer layer of 77% copper, 12% zinc, 7% manganese, and 4% nickel, bonded to a pure copper core.

Weight: 8.1 grams / 0.28 oz.

Important dates: 2007, Washington, Plain Edge; 2007, Adams, Plain Edge; 2007, Jefferson, Plain Edge.

2007, G. Washington.

2007, J. Adams.

2007, Jefferson.

2007, Madison.

2008, Monroe.

2008, J.Q. Adams.

2008, Jackson.

2008, Van Buren.

2009, W.H. Harrison.

2009, Tyler.

2009, Polk.

2009, Taylor.

2010, Fillmore.

2010, Pierce.

2010, Buchanan.

2010, Lincoln.

2011, Johnson.

2011, Grant.

2011, Hayes.

2011, Garfield.

2012, Arthur.

2012, Cleveland,
variety 1.

2012, B. Harrison.

2012, Cleveland,
variety 2.

2013, McKinley.   2013, T. Roosevelt.   2013, Taft.   2013, Wilson.

2014, Harding.   2014, Coolidge.   2014, Hoover.   2014, F. Roosevelt.

SILVER U.S. COINS
SHIELD/STAR THREE-CENT PIECE (1851–1873)

Actual size:
14 mm / 0.55 in.

Obverse: Union shield centered in a six-pointed star, by James B. Longacre.

Reverse: Roman numeral III centered in a large stylized C, by James B. Longacre.

Edge: Plain.

Mintmark: O, in right field of reverse, only in 1851.

Metallic content: (1851–1853) 75% silver, 25% copper.

(1854–1873) 90% silver, 10% copper.

Weights: (1851–1853) 0.80 grams / 0.03 oz. (1854–1873) 0.75 grams / 0.02 oz.

Actual silver weights: (1851–1853) 0.60 grams / 0.02 oz. (1854–1873) 0.67 grams / 0.02 oz.

Important dates: All dates from 1863 through 1873.

SILVER

FLOWING HAIR HALF DIME (1792 PATTERN, 1794–1795)

Actual size:
16.5 mm / 0.65 in.

Obverse: Flowing Hair, by Robert Scot.
Reverse: Small Eagle, by Robert Scot.
Edge: Reeded.
Mintmark: None (all struck at the Philadelphia Mint).

Metallic content: 89.25% silver, 10.75% copper.
Weight: 1.348 grams / 0.05 oz.
Actual silver weight: 1.2 grams / 0.04 oz.
Important dates: 1792 pattern is exceedingly rare; 1794; 1795.

DRAPED BUST HALF DIME (1796–1805)

Actual size:
16.5 mm / 0.65 in.

Obverse: Draped bust of Liberty, designed by Gilbert Stuart, engraved by Robert Scot.
Reverses: (1796–1797) Small Eagle, by Robert Scot. (1800–1805) Heraldic Eagle, by Robert Scot.
Edge: Reeded.
Mintmark: None (all struck at the Philadelphia Mint).

Metallic content: 89.25% silver, 10.75% copper.
Weight: 1.35 grams / 0.05 oz.
Actual silver weight: 1.2 grams / 0.04 oz.
Important dates: 1797, 13 Stars; 1802; 1803, Small 8.

CAPPED BUST HALF DIME (1829–1837)

Actual size:
15.5 mm / 0.61 in.

Obverse: Capped bust of Liberty, by John Reich.
Reverse: Eagle with shield on breast, by John Reich.
Edge: Reeded.
Mintmark: None (all struck at the Philadelphia Mint).

Metallic content: 89.25% silver, 10.75% copper.
Weight: 1.35 grams / 0.05 oz.
Actual silver weight: 1.2 grams / 0.04 oz.
Important date: 1837, Small 5c.

LIBERTY SEATED HALF DIME (1837–1873)

Actual size:
15.5 mm / 0.61 in.

Obverse: Seated Liberty, by Christian Gobrecht.
Reverse: Cereal wreath with HALF DIME in the center, by Christian Gobrecht.
Edge: Reeded.
Mintmarks: O, S, on the reverse, within or below the wreath.
Metallic content: 90% silver, 10% copper.

Weights: (1837–1853) 1.34 grams / 0.05 oz. (1853–1873) 1.24 grams / 0.04 oz.
Actual silver weights: (1837–1853) 1.20 grams / 0.04 oz. (1853–1873) 1.12 grams / 0.04 oz.
Important dates: 1838-O, No Stars; 1846, With Drapery; 1853-O, With Drapery; 1867.

DRAPED BUST DIME (1796–1807)

Actual size:
18.8 mm / 0.74 in.

Obverse: Draped bust of Liberty, by Gilbert Stuart.
Reverses: (1796–1797) Small Eagle, by Robert Scot. (1798–1807) Heraldic Eagle, by Robert Scot.
Edge: Reeded.
Mintmark: None (all struck at the Philadelphia Mint).

Metallic content: 89.25% silver, 10.75% copper.
Weight: 2.7 grams / 0.09 oz.
Actual silver weight: 2.41 grams / 0.08 oz.
Important dates: 1798, 8 Over 7, 13 Stars on Reverse; 1804, 14 Stars on Reverse.

CAPPED BUST DIME (1809–1837)

Actual size:
(1809–1828)
18.8 mm / 0.74 in.
(1828–1837)
17.9 mm / 0.71 in.

Obverse: Capped bust of Liberty, by John Reich.
Reverse: Eagle with shield on breast, by John Reich.
Edge: Reeded.
Mintmark: None (all struck at the Philadelphia Mint).

Metallic content: 89.25% silver, 10.75% copper.
Weight: 2.7 grams / 0.09 oz.
Actual silver weight: 2.41 grams / 0.08 oz.
Important date: 1822.

LIBERTY SEATED DIME (1837–1891)

Actual size:
17.9 mm / 0.71 in.

Obverses: (1837–1840) Seated Liberty, by Christian Gobrecht. (1840–1860) Seated Liberty, by Christian Gobrecht, modified by Robert Ball Hughes. (1860–1891) Seated Liberty, by Gobrecht.
Reverses: (1840–1860) Wreath with ONE DIME in the center, by Christian Gobrecht. (1860–1891) Cereal wreath with ONE DIME in the center, by James B. Longacre.
Edge: Reeded.
Mintmarks: O, S, CC, on the reverse, within and below the wreath.

Metallic content: 90% silver, 10% copper.
Weights: (1837–1853) 2.40 grams / 0.08 oz. (1853–1873) 2.49 grams / 0.09 oz. (1873–1874) 2.50 grams / 0.09 oz. (1875–1891) 2.49 grams / 0.09 oz.
Actual silver weights: (1837–1853) 2.40 grams / 0.08 oz. (1853–1873) 2.24 grams / 0.07 oz. (1873–1874) 2.25 grams / 0.07 oz. (1875–1891) 2.24 grams / 0.07 oz.
Important dates: 1871-CC, Legend Obverse; 1873-CC, Arrows at Date; 1874-CC, Arrows at Date.

BARBER DIME (1892–1916)

Actual size:
17.9 mm / 0.71 in.

Obverse: Liberty Head, by Charles Barber.
Reverse: Cereal wreath with ONE DIME in the center, by James B. Longacre.
Edge: Reeded.
Mintmarks: O, S, D, on the reverse, below the bow in the wreath.

Metallic content: 90% silver, 10% copper.
Weight: 2.5 grams / 0.09 oz.
Actual silver weight: 2.25 grams / 0.07 oz.
Important dates: Proof 1894-S; 1895-O; 1903-S.

WINGED LIBERTY HEAD (MERCURY) DIME (1916–1945)

Actual size:
17.9 mm / 0.71 in.

Obverse: Winged Liberty Head, by Adolph Weinman.
Reverse: Roman fasces (ax blade bound into a bundle of rods secured by bands), by Adolph Weinman.
Edge: Reeded.
Mintmarks: D, S, on the reverse, to the left at the base of the fasces.

Metallic content: 90% silver, 10% copper.
Weight: 2.5 grams / 0.09 oz.
Actual silver weight: 2.25 grams / 0.07 oz.
Important dates: 1916-D; 1921; 1921-D; 1942, 2 Over 1; 1942-D, 42 Over 41.

ROOSEVELT DIME (1946 TO DATE)

Actual size:
17.9 mm / 0.71 in.

Obverse: Portrait of Franklin D. Roosevelt, by John R. Sinnock.
Reverse: Flaming torch, by John R. Sinnock.
Edge: Reeded.
Mintmarks: (1946–1964) D, S, on reverse, on left, at base of torch. (1968–1980) D, S, on obverse, above date. (1981 to date) P, D, S, on obverse, above date.
Metallic content: (1946–1964) 90% silver, 10% copper. (1965 to date) 75% copper, 25% nickel. (1992 to date) Silver Proofs, 90% silver, 10% copper.
Weights: (1946–1964, Silver Proofs 1992 to date) 2.50 grams / 0.09 oz. (1965 to date) 2.27 grams / 0.07 oz.
Actual silver weight: (1946–1964, Silver Proofs 1992 to date) 2.25 grams / 0.07 oz.
Important dates: 1975-S, No S; 1982, No Mintmark.

LIBERTY SEATED TWENTY-CENT PIECE (1875–1876)

Actual size:
22.5 mm / 0.89 in.

Obverse: Seated Liberty, by William Barber.
Reverse: Standing eagle with wings outstretched, by William Barber.
Edge: Plain.
Mintmarks: CC, S, on the reverse, centered below the eagle's talons.

Metallic content: 90% silver, 10% copper.
Weight: 5 grams / 0.16 oz.
Actual silver weight: 4.5 grams / 0.14 oz.
Important dates: 1876-CC; Proofs bearing dates of 1877 and 1878.

DRAPED BUST QUARTER DOLLAR (1796, 1804–1807)

Actual size: ~27.5 mm / ~1.07 in.

Obverse: Draped bust of Liberty, by Gilbert Stuart, engraved by Robert Scot.
Reverses: (1796) Small Eagle, by John Eckstein / Robert Scot. (1804–1807) Heraldic Eagle, by Robert Scot.
Edge: Reeded.

Mintmark: None (all struck at the Philadelphia Mint).
Metallic content: 89.25% silver, 10.75% copper.
Weight: 6.74 grams / 0.22 oz.
Actual silver weight: 6.02 grams / 0.19 oz.
Important dates: 1796; 1804.

CAPPED BUST QUARTER DOLLAR (1815–1838)

Actual size:
(1815–1828)
27 mm / 1.07 in.
(1831–1838)
24.26 mm / 0.96 in.

Obverse: Capped bust of Liberty, by John Reich.
Reverse: Eagle with downward-pointed wings, with shield on breast, by John Reich.
Edge: Reeded.
Mintmark: None (all struck at the Philadelphia Mint).

Metallic content: 89.25% silver, 10.75% copper.
Weight: 6.74 grams / 0.23 oz.
Actual silver weight: 6.02 grams / 0.19 oz.
Important dates: 1822, 25 Over 50c; 1823, 3 Over 2.

LIBERTY SEATED QUARTER DOLLAR (1838–1891)

Actual size:
24.26 mm / 0.96 in.

Obverses: (1838–1840) Seated Liberty, by Christian Gobrecht. (1840–1891) Seated Liberty, by Christian Gobrecht.
Reverses: (1838–1840) Eagle with downward-pointed wings, with shield on breast, by John Reich, modified by Christian Gobrecht and James B. Longacre. (1840–1891) Eagle with downward-pointed wings, with shield on breast, modified by Robert B. Hughes / Gobrecht / Longacre.
Edge: Reeded.
Mintmarks: O, S, CC, centered below the eagle's talons.

Metallic content: 90% silver, 10% copper.
Weights: (1838–1873) 6.22 grams / 0.22 oz. (1873–1891) 6.25 grams / 0.22 oz.
Actual silver weights: (1838–1873) 5.60 grams / 0.18 oz. (1873–1891) 5.63 grams / 0.18 oz.
Important dates: 1840-O, Large O; 1842-O, Small Date; 1843-O, Large O; 1849-O; 1854-O, Huge O; 1860-S; 1864-S; 1870-CC; 1871-CC; 1872-CC; 1872-S; 1873-CC; 1886.

BARBER QUARTER DOLLAR (1892–1916)

Actual size: 24.26 mm / 0.96 in.

Obverse: Head of Liberty, by Charles Barber.
Reverse: Eagle with wings spread, with shield on breast, by Charles Barber.
Edge: Reeded.
Mintmarks: O, S, D, on the reverse, below the eagle's tail feathers.

Metallic content: 90% silver, 10% copper.
Weight: 6.25 grams / 0.22 oz.
Actual silver weight: 5.63 grams / 0.18 oz.
Important dates: 1896-S; 1901-S; 1913-S; all Proofs.

STANDING LIBERTY QUARTER DOLLAR (1916–1930)

Actual size:
24.26 mm / 0.96 in.

Obverse: Standing Liberty, by Hermon MacNeil.
Reverse: Flying eagle, by Hermon MacNeil.
Edge: Reeded.
Mintmarks: S, D, on the obverse, to the left of the date.

Metallic content: 90% silver, 10% copper.
Weight: 6.25 grams / 0.22 oz.
Actual silver weight: 5.63 grams / 0.18 oz.
Important dates: 1916; 1918, 18 Over 17; 1921; 1923-S.

WASHINGTON QUARTER DOLLAR (1932 TO DATE)

Actual size:
24.26 mm / 0.96 in.

1776–1976
Bicentennial reverse.

1999 to date, Statehood, Territorial, and National Park obverse.

See the following pages for illustrations of all Statehood, Territorial, and National Park quarters issued to date.

SILVER

Obverse: George Washington portrait, by John Flanagan.
Reverses: (1932–1974) Full-figure heraldic eagle standing on a bundle of arrows, by John Flanagan. (1975–1976) Dual date of 1776–1976; military drummer, by Jack L. Ahr. (1977–1998) Full-figure heraldic eagle standing on a bundle of arrows, by Flanagan. (1999–2008) Statehood symbols, by various designers. (2009) Symbols of District of Columbia and U.S. territories, by various designers. (2010–2021) America the Beautiful [National Park] motifs, by various designers.
Edge: Reeded.
Mintmarks: (1932–1964) D, S, on the reverse, below the bow in the wreath; (1968 to date) D, S, P, on the obverse, to the right of the ribbon in Washington's queue (ponytail).
Metallic content: (1932–1964, and silver Proofs 1992 to date) 90% silver, 10% copper. (1976, Bicentennial Proofs and Uncirculated sets) Outer layer of 80% silver and 20% copper bonded to a core of 21.5% silver, 78.5% copper. (1965 to date) Outer layer of 75% copper and 25% nickel bonded to a pure copper core.
Weights: (1932–1964, and silver Proofs 1992 to date) 6.25 grams / 0.22 oz. (1976 Bicentennial Proof and Uncirculated sets) 5.75 grams / 0.20 oz. (1965 to date) 5.67 grams / 0.20 oz.
Actual silver weights: (1932–1964, and silver Proofs 1992 to date) 5.63 grams / 0.18 oz. (1976 Bicentennial Proof and Uncirculated sets) 2.30 grams / 0.07 oz.
Important dates: 1932-D; 1932-S; 1934, Doubled Die Obverse; 1937, Doubled Die Obverse; 1942-D, Doubled Die Obverse; 1942-D, Doubled Die Obverse; 1943, Doubled Die Obverse; 1943-S, Doubled Die Obverse; 2004-D, Wisconsin, Extra Leaf High; 2004-D, Wisconsin, Extra Leaf Low.

1999, Delaware.

1999, Pennsylvania.

1999, New Jersey.

1999, Georgia.

1999, Connecticut.

2000,
Massachusetts.

2000,
Maryland.

2000,
South Carolina.

2000, New
Hampshire.

2000,
Virginia.

2001,
New York.

2001,
North Carolina.

2001,
Rhode Island.

2001,
Vermont.

2001,
Kentucky.

2002,
Tennessee.

2002,
Ohio.

2002,
Louisiana.

2002,
Indiana.

2002,
Mississippi.

2003,
Illinois.

2003,
Alabama.

2003,
Maine.

2003,
Missouri.

2003,
Arkansas.

SILVER

2004, Michigan.

2004, Florida.

2004, Texas.

2004, Iowa.

2004, Wisconsin.

2005, California.

2005, Minnesota.

2005, Oregon.

2005, Kansas.

2005, West Virginia.

2006, Nevada.

2006, Nebraska.

2006, Colorado.

2006, North Dakota.

2006, South Dakota.

2007, Montana.

2007, Washington.

2007, Idaho.

2007, Wyoming.

2007, Utah.

2008, Oklahoma.

2008, New Mexico.

2008, Arizona.

2008, Alaska.

2008, Hawaii.

2009, District of Columbia.

2009, Puerto Rico.

2009, Guam.

2009, American Samoa.

2009, U.S. Virgin Islands.

2009, Northern Mariana Islands.

2010, Hot Springs National Park (AR).

2010, Yellowstone National Park (WY).

2010, Yosemite National Park (CA).

2010, Grand Canyon National Park (AZ).

2010, Mt. Hood National Forest (OR).

2011, Gettysburg National Military Park (PA).

2011, Glacier National Park (MT).

2011, Olympic National Park (WA).

2011, Vicksburg National Military Park (MS).

2011, Chickasaw National Recreation Area (OK).

SILVER

2012, El Yunque National Forest (PR).

2012, Chaco Culture National Historical Park (NM).

2012, Acadia National Park (ME).

2012, Hawai'i Volcanoes National Park (HI).

2012, Denali National Park and Preserve (AK).

2013, White Mountain National Forest (NH).

2013, Perry's Victory and Internat'l Peace Memorial (OH).

2013, Great Basin National Park (NV).

2013, Fort McHenry National Monument and Historic Shrine (MD).

2013, Mount Rushmore National Memorial (SD).

2014, Great Smoky Mountains National Park (TN).

2014, Shenandoah National Park (VA).

2014, Arches National Park (UT).

2014, Great Sand Dunes National Park (CO).

2014, Everglades National Park (FL).

FLOWING HAIR HALF DOLLAR (1794–1795)

Actual size:
32.5 mm / 1.28 in.

Obverse: Liberty with flowing hair, by Robert Scot.
Reverse: Small Eagle, by Robert Scot.
Edges: Lettered FIFTY CENTS, or HALF A DOLLAR.
Mintmark: None (all struck at the Philadelphia Mint).

Metallic content: 90% silver, 10% copper.
Weight: 13.48 grams / 0.47 oz.
Actual silver weight: 12.13 grams / 0.39 oz.
Important dates: All are rare. Key dates are 1794; 1795, Silver Plug.

DRAPED BUST HALF DOLLAR (1796–1797, 1801–1807)

Actual size:
32.5 mm / 1.28 in.

Obverse: Liberty with a draped bust, by Robert Scot.
Reverses: (1796–1797) Small Eagle, by Robert Scot. (1801–1807) Heraldic Eagle, by Robert Scot.
Edges: Lettered FIFTY CENTS, or HALF A DOLLAR.
Mintmarks: None (all struck at the Philadelphia Mint).

Metallic content: 89.25% silver, 10.75% copper.
Weight: 13.48 grams / 0.47 oz.
Actual silver weight: 12.03 grams / 0.39 oz.
Important dates: 1796, 15 Stars; 1796, 16 Stars; 1797; 1806, Knobbed 6, No Stem.

SILVER

CAPPED BUST HALF DOLLAR (1807–1839)

Actual size:
(1807–1836)
32.5 mm / 1.28 in.
(1836–1839)
30.61 mm / 1.21 in.

Obverse: Capped bust of Liberty, by John Reich.

Reverses: (1807–1836) Eagle with downward-pointed wings, and shield on breast, by John Reich. (1836–1839) John Reich / Christian Gobrecht.

Edges: (1807–1836) Lettered, FIFTY CENTS, or HALF A DOLLAR. (1836–1839) Reeded.

Mintmark: O, on obverse, above the date (only for 1838 and 1839).

Metallic content: (1807–1836) 89.25% silver, 10.75% copper. (1836–1839) 90% silver, 10% copper.

Weights: (1807–1836) 13.48 grams / 0.47 oz. (1836–1839) 13.37 grams / 0.43 oz.

Actual silver weights: (1807–1836) 12.03 grams / 0.39 oz. (1836–1839) 12.03 grams / 0.39 oz.

Important dates: 1821, 2 Over 1, Large 8; 1815, 5 Over 2; 1830, Large Letters; 1836.

LIBERTY SEATED HALF DOLLAR (1839–1891)

Actual size:
30.61 mm / 1.21 in.

Obverse: Seated Liberty, by Christian Gobrecht.
Reverse: Eagle with downward-pointed wings, and shield on breast, by John Reich / Christian Gobrecht.
Edge: Reeded.
Mintmarks: O, S, CC, on the reverse center, below the eagle.
Metallic content: 90% silver, 10% copper.
Weights: (1839–1853) 13.37 grams / 0.47 oz. (1853–1873)

12.40 grams / 0.43 oz. (1873–1891) 12.5 grams / 0.44 oz.
Actual silver weights: (1839–1853) 12.03 grams / 0.39 oz. (1853–1873) 11.20 grams / 0.36 oz. (1873–1891) 11.25 grams / 0.36 oz.
Important dates: 1847, 7 Over 6; 1853-O, Modified Reverse, Large Letters; 1870-CC; 1873, Open 3; 1878-S.

BARBER HALF DOLLAR (1892–1915)

Actual size:
30.61 mm / 1.21 in.

Obverse: Head of Liberty, by Charles Barber.
Reverse: Heraldic Eagle, by Charles Barber.
Edge: Reeded.
Mintmarks: O, S, D, on reverse, below the eagle's tail feathers.

Metallic content: 90% silver, 10% copper.
Weight: 12.5 grams / 0.44 oz.
Actual silver weight: 11.25 grams / 0.36 oz.
Important dates: 1892-O; 1892-O, Micro O; 1892-S; 1893-S; 1897-O; 1914.

LIBERTY WALKING HALF DOLLAR (1916–1947)

Actual size:
30.61 mm / 1.21 in.

Obverse: Walking Liberty, by Adolph Weinman.
Reverse: Standing eagle, by Adolph Weinman.
Edge: Reeded.
Mintmarks: (1916) S, D, on obverse, below IN GOD WE TRUST. (1917) S, D, on obverse, below IN GOD WE TRUST, or on reverse, at 8 o'clock position.
(1918–1947) S, D, on reverse, at the 8 o'clock position.
Metallic content: 90% silver, 10% copper.
Weight: 12.5 grams / 0.44 oz.
Actual silver weight: 11.25 grams / 0.36 oz.
Important dates: 1916-S; 1921; 1921-D; 1921-S; 1946, Doubled Die Reverse.

FRANKLIN HALF DOLLAR (1948–1963)

Actual size:
30.61 mm / 1.21 in.

Obverse: Portrait of Benjamin Franklin, by John Sinnock.
Reverse: Liberty Bell, by John Sinnock.
Edge: Reeded.
Mintmarks: S, D, on reverse, centered above the beam from which the bell is hanging.
Metallic content: 90% silver, 10% copper.
Weight: 12.5 grams / 0.44 oz.
Actual silver weight: 11.25 grams / 0.36 oz.
Important dates: 1949-D; 1949-S; 1952-S.

KENNEDY HALF DOLLAR (1964 TO DATE)

Actual size:
30.61 mm / 1.21 in.

Obverse: Portrait of John F. Kennedy, by Gilroy Roberts.
Reverses: (1964–1974) Heraldic eagle from presidential seal, by Frank Gasparro. (1776–1976 Bicentennial) Independence Hall, by Seth G. Huntington. (1977 to date) Heraldic eagle from presidential seal, by Frank Gasparro.
Edge: Reeded.
Mintmarks: (1964) D, on reverse, near the eagle's talon holding the olive branch. (1968–1979) D, S, on obverse, below Kennedy's neck. (1980 to date) P, D, S, on obverse, below Kennedy's neck.
Metallic content: (1964, and silver Proofs 1992 to date) 90% silver, 10% copper. (1965–1970) Outer layer of 80% silver and 20% copper bonded to a core of 21.5% silver, 78.5% copper [net 40% silver]. (1976 Bicentennial Proof and Uncirculated sets) Outer layer of 80% silver, 20% copper bonded to a core of 21.5% silver, 78.5% copper [net 40%

1776–1976
Bicentennial reverse.

silver]. (1971 to date) Outer layer of 75% copper, 25% nickel bonded to a pure copper core.
Weights: (1964, and silver Proofs 1992 to date) 12.50 grams / 0.44 oz. (1965–1970, and Bicentennial Proof and Uncirculated sets) 11.50 grams / 0.40 oz. (1971 to date) 11.34 grams / 0.40 oz.
Actual silver weights: (1964, and silver Proofs 1992 to date) 11.25 grams / 0.36 oz. (1965–1970, and Bicentennial Proof and Uncirculated sets) 4.60 grams / 0.15 oz.
Important dates: 1964; 1964, Heavily Accented Hair; 1964-D.

SILVER

FLOWING HAIR DOLLAR (1794–1795)

Shown actual size
(39.5 mm / 1.56 in.).

Obverse: Liberty with flowing hair, by Robert Scot.

Reverse: Small Eagle, by Robert Scot.

Edge: Lettered (HUNDRED CENTS or ONE DOLLAR or ONE UNIT).

Mintmark: None (all struck at the Philadelphia Mint).

Metallic content: 89.24% silver, 10.76% copper.

Weight: 26.96 grams / 0.95 oz.

Actual silver weight: 26.96 grams / 0.87 oz.

Important dates: All are rare. Key date: 1794.

DRAPED BUST DOLLAR (1795–1803)

Shown actual size
(39.5 mm / 1.56 in.).

Obverse: Liberty with draped bust, by Robert Scot.
Reverse: (1795–1798) Small Eagle, by Robert Scot. (1798–1803) Heraldic Eagle, by Robert Scot.
Edge: Lettered (HUNDRED CENTS or ONE DOLLAR or ONE UNIT).
Mintmark: None (all struck at the Philadelphia Mint).
Metallic content: 89.25% silver, 10.75% copper.

Weight: 26.96 grams / 0.95 oz.
Actual silver weight: 24.06 grams / 0.77 oz.
Important dates: All are rare. Key dates: 1795, Centered Bust; 1795, Off-Center Bust; 1797, 9 Stars Left, 7 Stars Right, Small Letters; 1798, 15 Obverse Stars; 1802, 2 Over 1, Wide Date; 1804, originals and 1804 restrikes.

LIBERTY SEATED DOLLAR (1840–1873)

Shown actual size (38.1 mm / 1.5 in.).

Obverse: Seated Liberty, by Christian Gobrecht.
Reverse: Eagle with downward-pointed wings, and shield on breast, by Christian Gobrecht.
Edge: Reeded.
Mintmarks: O, S, CC, on reverse, centered below the eagle's talons.

Metallic content: 90% silver, 10% copper.
Weight: 26.73 grams / 0.94 oz.
Actual silver weight: 24.06 grams / 0.77 oz.
Important dates: 1854; 1871-CC; 1872-CC; 1873-CC.

TRADE DOLLAR (1873–1885)

Shown actual size
(38.1 mm / 1.5 in.).

Obverse: Liberty seated, extending an olive branch in her right hand, by Charles Barber.
Reverse: Eagle with downward-pointed wings, by Charles Barber.
Edge: Reeded.
Mintmarks: S, CC, on reverse, above TRADE DOLLAR.

Metallic content: 90% silver, 10% copper.
Weight: 27.22 grams / 0.96 oz.
Actual silver weight: 24.49 grams / 0.79 oz.
Important dates: Proofs of 1878, 1879, 1880, 1881, 1882, 1883, 1884, and 1885.

MORGAN DOLLAR (1878–1921)

Shown actual size
(38.1 mm / 1.5 in.).

Obverse: Head of Liberty, by George Morgan.
Reverse: Eagle with outstretched wings, by George Morgan.
Edge: Reeded.
Mintmarks: O, CC, S, D, on reverse, centered below the bow in the wreath.
Metallic content: 90% silver, 10% copper.

Weight: 26.73 grams / 0.94 oz.
Actual silver weight: 24.06 grams / 0.77 oz.
Important dates: 1879-CC; 1881-CC; 1885-CC; 1889-CC; 1893-S; 1895, Proof; 1895-O; 1895-S; 1903-O.

PEACE DOLLAR (1921–1935)

Shown actual size
(38.1 mm / 1.5 in.).

Obverse: Head of Liberty, with rays, by Anthony de Francisci.
Reverse: Eagle standing on a rock, by Anthony de Francisci.
Edge: Reeded.
Mintmarks: D, S, on reverse, on the left, near the rim, above the eagle's wing and below ONE legend.

Metallic content: 90% silver, 10% copper.
Weight: 26.73 grams / 0.94 oz.
Actual silver weight: 24.06 grams / 0.77 oz.
Important dates: 1921; 1923, Tail O; 1928; 1934-D, Doubled Die Obverse, Micro D; 1934-S.

SILVER

EISENHOWER DOLLAR (1971–1978)

Shown actual size
(38.1 mm / 1.5 in.).

1776–1976
Bicentennial reverse.

Obverse: Portrait of Dwight D. Eisenhower, by Frank Gasparro.
Reverses: (1971–1974) Eagle landing on the moon, by Frank Gasparro. (1975 and 1976, dated 1776–1976) Liberty Bell superimposed on the moon, by

Dennis R. Williams. (1977–1978) Eagle landing on the moon, by Frank Gasparro.
Edge: Reeded.
Mintmarks: D, S, on obverse, below Eisenhower's neck and above the date.

Metallic content: (1971–1978) Outer layer of 75% copper and 25% nickel bonded to a pure copper core. (1971–1974) Outer layer of 80% silver and 20% copper bonded to core of 21.5% silver and 78.5% copper [net 40% silver]. (1976 Bicentennial Proofs and Uncirculated sets) Outer layer of 80% silver and 20% copper bonded to a core of 21.5% silver and 78.5% copper [net 40% silver].

Weights: (Copper-nickel) 22.68 grams / 0.80 oz. (40% silver) 24.59 grams / 0.86 oz.
Actual silver weight: 9.84 grams / 0.32 oz.
Important dates: 1971-S; 1972-S; 1973-S; 1974-S.
Note: Grade rarity is a factor for many dates in grades MS-65 and above.

GOLD U.S. COINS
LIBERTY HEAD GOLD DOLLAR (1849–1854)

Actual size:
13 mm / 0.51 in.

Obverse: Head of Liberty wearing a coronet, by James B. Longacre.
Reverse: Laurel wreath encircling the numeral 1, by James B. Longacre and Peter Filatreu Cross.
Edge: Reeded.
Mintmarks: C, D, O, S, on reverse, below the knot in the bow binding the laurel wreath.

Metallic content: 90% gold, 10% copper and silver.
Weight: 1.67 grams / 0.05 oz.
Actual gold weight: 1.5 grams / 0.05 oz.
Important dates: 1849-C, Closed Wreath; 1849-C, Open Wreath; 1849-D; 1851-D; 1852-D; 1853-D.

INDIAN PRINCESS HEAD GOLD DOLLAR (1854–1889)

Actual size:
14.86 mm / 0.59 in.

Obverses: (1854–1856) Indian Princess Head, Small Head, by James B. Longacre. (1856–1889) Indian Princess Head, Large Head, by James B. Longacre. **Reverse:** Agricultural wreath encircling the numeral, 1 by James B. Longacre. **Edge:** Reeded. **Mintmarks:** C, D, O, S, on reverse, below the knot in the bow binding the agricultural wreath.

Metallic content: 90% gold, 10% copper and silver. **Weight:** 1.67 grams / 0.05 oz. **Actual silver weight:** 1.5 grams / 0.05 oz. **Important dates:** 1855-C; 1855-D; 1856-D; 1857-C; 1857-D; 1858-D; 1859-C; 1859-D; 1860-D; 1861-D; 1875.

CAPPED BUST TO RIGHT QUARTER EAGLE ($2.50) (1796–1807)

Actual size:
20 mm / 0.79 in.

Obverse: Capped bust of Liberty, by Robert Scot.
Reverse: Heraldic eagle from the Great Seal of the United States, by Robert Scot.
Edge: Reeded.
Mintmark: None (all struck at the Philadelphia Mint).
Metallic content: 91.67% gold, 8.33% copper and silver.

Weight: 4.37 grams / 0.15 oz.
Actual silver weight: 4.01 grams / 0.13 oz.
Important dates: All are rare. 1796, No Stars on Obverse; 1796, Stars on Obverse; 1797; 1804, 13 Stars on Reverse.

CAPPED BUST TO LEFT QUARTER EAGLE ($2.50) (1808)

Actual size:
20 mm / 0.79 in.

Obverse: Capped draped bust of Liberty, by John Reich.
Reverse: Eagle with shield on breast, by John Reich.
Edge: Reeded.
Mintmark: None (all struck at the Philadelphia Mint).

Metallic content: 91.67% gold, 8.33% copper and silver.
Weight: 4.37 grams / 0.15 oz.
Actual gold weight: 4.01 grams / 0.13 oz.
Important date: 1808.

CAPPED HEAD TO LEFT QUARTER EAGLE ($2.50) (1821–1834)

Actual size:
(1821–1827)
18.5 mm / 0.73 in.
(1829–1834)
18.2 mm / 0.72 in.

Obverse: Capped bust of Liberty, by John Reich.
Reverse: Eagle with shield on breast, by John Reich.
Edge: Reeded.
Mintmark: None (all struck at the Philadelphia Mint).

Metallic content: 91.67% gold, 8.33% copper and silver.
Weight: 4.37 grams / 0.15 oz.
Actual gold weight: 4.01 grams / 0.13 oz.
Important dates: 1826, 6 Over 6; 1834, With Motto.

CLASSIC HEAD QUARTER EAGLE ($2.50) (1834–1839)

Actual size:
18.2 mm / 0.72 in.

Obverse: Classic head of Liberty, by William Kneass.
Reverse: Eagle with shield on breast, without motto, by William Kneass.
Edge: Reeded.
Mintmarks: C, D, O, only during 1838 and 1839, on the obverse, above the date.

Metallic content: (1834–1836) 89.92% gold, 10.08% copper and silver. (1837–1839) 90% gold, 10% copper and silver.
Weight: 4.18 grams / 0.14 oz.
Actual gold weights: (1834–1836) 3.758 grams / 0.12 oz. (1837–1839) 3.762 grams / 0.12 oz.
Important dates: 1838-C; 1839-C; 1839-D.

GOLD

LIBERTY HEAD QUARTER EAGLE ($2.50) (1840–1907)

Actual size:
18.2 mm / 0.72 in.

Obverse: Head of Liberty wearing a coronet, by Christian Gobrecht.
Reverse: Eagle with shield on breast, without motto, by Christian Gobrecht.
Edge: Reeded.
Mintmarks: C, D, O, S, on reverse, below the eagle's talons.

Metallic content: 90% gold, 10% copper and silver.
Weight: 4.18 grams / 0.14 oz.
Actual gold weight: 3.76 grams / 0.12 oz.
Important dates: 1848, CAL.; 1854-S; 1864; 1865; 1875.

INDIAN HEAD QUARTER EAGLE ($2.50) (1908–1929)

Actual size:
17.78 mm / 0.7 in.

Obverse: Male Indian wearing a war bonnet, by Bela Lyon Pratt.
Reverse: Eagle perched atop a bundle of arrows, holding an olive sprig in its right talon, by Augustus Saint-Gaudens.
Edge: Reeded.

Mintmark: D, on reverse, near the left rim, below the olive leaves.
Metallic content: 90% gold, 10% copper.
Weight: 4.18 grams / 0.14 oz.
Actual gold weight: 3.76 grams / 0.12 oz.
Important date: 1911-D.

INDIAN HEAD THREE-DOLLAR GOLD PIECE (1854–1889)

Actual size:
20.5 mm / 0.81 in.

Obverse: Liberty as an Indian wearing a headdress, by James B. Longacre.

Reverse: Agricultural wreath encircling 3 DOLLARS, by James B. Longacre.

Edge: Reeded.

Mintmarks: D, O, S, on reverse, below the knot in the bow.

Metallic content: (1854–1873) 90% gold, 10% copper and silver. (1873–1889) 90% gold, 10% copper.

Weight: 5.02 grams / 0.17 oz.

Actual gold weight: 4.51 grams / 0.14 oz.

Important dates: 1854-D; 1875, Proof; 1876, Proof.

CAPPED BUST TO RIGHT HALF EAGLE ($5) (1795–1807)

Actual size:
25 mm / 0.99 in.

GOLD

Obverse: Capped bust of Liberty, by Robert Scot.
Reverses: (1795–1798) Small eagle, by Robert Scot. (1798–1807) Heraldic eagle from the Great Seal of the United States, by Robert Scot.
Edge: Reeded.
Mintmark: None (all struck at the Philadelphia Mint).

Metallic content: 91.67% gold, 8.33% copper and silver.
Weight: 8.75 grams / 0.3 oz.
Actual gold weight: 8.02 grams / 0.26 oz.
Important dates: All are rare. Small Eagle Reverse: 1795; 1796, 6 Over 5; 1797, 15 Stars on Obverse; 1797, 16 Stars on Obverse; 1798.

CAPPED BUST TO LEFT HALF EAGLE ($5) (1807–1812)

Actual size:
25 mm / 0.99 in.

Obverse: Capped bust of Liberty, by John Reich.
Reverse: Heraldic eagle, by John Reich.
Edge: Reeded.
Mintmark: None (all struck at the Philadelphia Mint).
Metallic content: 91.67% gold, 8.33% copper and silver.

Weight: 8.75 grams / 0.3 oz.
Actual gold weight: 8.02 grams / 0.26 oz.
Important dates: 1810, Small Date, Small 5; 1810, Large Date, Small 5.

CAPPED HEAD TO LEFT HALF EAGLE ($5) (1813–1834)

Actual size:
(1813–1829)
25 mm / 0.99 in.
(1829–1834)
22.5 mm / 0.89 in.

Obverse: Capped draped bust of Liberty, by John Reich.
Reverse: Eagle with a shield on its breast, by John Reich.
Edge: Reeded.
Mintmark: None (all struck at the Philadelphia Mint).
Metallic content: 91.67% gold, 8.33% copper and silver.
Weight: 8.75 grams / 0.3 oz.

Actual gold weight: 8.02 grams / 0.26 oz.
Important dates: All are rare. 1819, Wide Date; 1819, Close Date; 1829, Large Planchet; 1829, Small Planchet; 1832, Curl Base 2, 12 Stars; 1832, Square Base 2, 13 Stars; 1833, Large Date; 1833, Small Date.

CLASSIC HEAD HALF EAGLE ($5) (1834–1838)

Actual size:
22.5 mm / 0.89 in.

GOLD

Obverse: Classic head of Liberty, by William Kneass.
Reverse: Eagle with a shield on its breast, without motto, by William Kneass.
Edge: Reeded.
Mintmarks: C, D, only during 1838, on obverse, above the date.
Metallic content: (1834–1836) 89.92% gold, 10.08% copper and silver. (1837–1838) 90% gold, 10% copper and silver.
Weight: 8.36 grams / 0.29 oz.
Actual gold weights: (1834–1836) 7.516 grams / 0.24 oz. (1837–1838) 7.523 grams / 0.24 oz.
Important dates: 1834, Crosslet 4; 1838-C; 1838-D.

LIBERTY HEAD HALF EAGLE ($5) (1839–1908)

Actual size:
(1839–1840)
22.5 mm / 0.89 in.
(1840–1908)
21.54 mm / 0.85 in.

Obverse: Head of Liberty wearing a coronet, by Christian Gobrecht.
Reverse: Eagle with a shield on its breast, by Christian Gobrecht.
Edge: Reeded.
Mintmarks: C, CC, D, O, S, on reverse, below the eagle's talons.
Metallic content: (1839–1849) 89.92% gold, 10.08% copper and silver. (1849–1908) 90% gold, 10% copper.
Weight: 8.36 grams / 0.29 oz.
Actual gold weight: 7.52 grams / 0.24 oz.
Important dates: 1842-C, Small Date; 1861-D; 1864-S; 1870-CC; 1873-CC; 1887, Proof.

INDIAN HEAD HALF EAGLE ($5) (1908–1929)

Actual size:
21.54 mm / 0.85 in.

Obverse: Male Indian wearing a war bonnet, by Bela Lyon Pratt.
Reverse: Eagle perched atop a bundle of arrows, holding an olive sprig in its right talon, by Augustus Saint-Gaudens.
Edge: Reeded
Mintmarks: D, O, S, on reverse, near the left rim, below the olive leaves.

Metallic content: 90% gold, 10% copper.
Weight: 8.36 grams / 0.29 oz.
Actual gold weight: 7.52 grams / 0.24 oz.
Important dates: 1909-O; 1929.

CAPPED BUST TO RIGHT EAGLE ($10) (1795–1804)

Actual size:
33 mm / 1.3 in.

Obverse: Capped bust of Liberty, by Robert Scot.
Reverses: (1795–1797) Small eagle, by Robert Scot. (1797–1804) Heraldic eagle, from the Great Seal of the United States, by Robert Scot.
Edge: Reeded.
Mintmark: None (all struck at the Philadelphia Mint).

Metallic content: 91.67% gold, 8.33% copper and silver.
Weight: 17.5 grams / 0.61 oz.
Actual gold weight: 16.04 grams / 0.52 oz.
Important dates: All are rare. 1795, 9 Leaves; 1796; 1797; 1798, 8 Over 7, 7 Stars Left, 6 Stars Right.

LIBERTY HEAD EAGLE ($10) (1838–1907)

Actual size:
27 mm / 1.07 in.

Obverse: Head of Liberty wearing a coronet, by Christian Gobrecht.
Reverse: Eagle with a shield on its breast, by Christian Gobrecht.
Edge: Reeded.
Mintmarks: CC, O, S, D, on reverse, below the eagle's talons.
Metallic content: (1838–1873) 90% gold, 10% copper and silver.

(1873–1907) 90% gold, 10% copper.
Weight: 17.72 grams / 0.62 oz.
Actual gold weight: 15.05 grams / 0.48 oz.
Important dates: 1841-O; 1858; 1863; 1865-S; 1865-S 865/ Inverted 186, 1870-CC, 1875, 1879-CC, 1883-O

INDIAN HEAD EAGLE ($10) (1907–1933)

Actual size:
27 mm / 1.07 in.

Obverse: Female wearing an Indian headdress, by Augustus Saint-Gaudens.
Reverse: Eagle perched atop a bundle of arrows, holding an olive sprig in its right talon, by Augustus Saint-Gaudens.
Edge: Stars.
Mintmarks: D, S, on reverse, near the rim, below the olive leaves.

Metallic content: 90% gold, 10% copper.
Weight: 16.72 grams / 0.59 oz.
Actual gold weight: 15.05 grams / 0.48 oz.
Important dates: 1907, Wire Rim, Periods; 1907, Rolled Rim, Periods; 1920-S; 1930-S; 1933.

LIBERTY HEAD DOUBLE EAGLE ($20) (1850–1907)

Actual size:
34.29 mm / 1.35 in.

GOLD

Obverse: Head of Liberty wearing a coronet, by James B. Longacre.
Reverse: Eagle with a shield on its breast by Gobrecht / John Reich / William Kneass.
Edge: Reeded.
Mintmarks: CC, O, S, D, on reverse, below the eagle's tail feathers.

Metallic content: (1850–1873) 90% gold, 10% copper and silver. (1873–1907) 90% gold, 10% copper.
Weight: 33.44 grams / 1.17 oz.
Actual gold weight: 30.09 grams / 0.97 oz.
Important dates: 1854-O; 1855-O; 1856-O; 1861-S, Paquet Reverse; 1870-CC.

SAINT-GAUDENS DOUBLE EAGLE ($20) (1907–1933)

Actual size:
34.29 mm / 1.35 in.

Obverse: Striding Liberty, by August Saint-Gaudens.
Reverse: Eagle in flight, by Augustus Saint-Gaudens.
Edge: Lettered (stars dividing words E PLURIBUS UNUM).
Mintmarks: D, S, on obverse, above the date.
Metallic content: 90% gold, 10% copper.

Weight: 33.47 grams / 1.18 oz.
Actual gold weight: 30.09 grams / 0.97 oz.
Important dates: 1907, High Relief, Roman Numerals, Wire Rim; 1907, High Relief, Roman Numerals, Flat Rim; 1920-S; 1921; 1927-D; 1930-S; 1933.

SILVER BULLION

AMERICA THE BEAUTIFUL 25¢ SILVER BULLION (2010–2021)

Shown actual size (76.2 mm / 3 in.)

SILVER
BULLION

Weight and purity incused on the edge.

Obverse: Portrait of George Washington, by John Flanagan.
Reverses: Same as reverse designs for America the Beautiful quarters (2010–2021). Designs by various artists, honoring 56 national parks and other national sites in each state, the District of Columbia, and five U.S. territories (Puerto Rico, Guam, American Samoa, the U.S. Virgin Islands, and the Northern Mariana Islands).
Edge: Lettered (.999 FINE SILVER 5.0 OUNCE).

Mintmark: P, on obverse, below IN GOD WE TRUST, only on Uncirculated collector version.
Metallic content: 99.9% silver, 0.1% copper.
Weight: 155.517 grams / 5 oz.
Actual silver weight: 155.517 grams / 5 oz.
Thickness: 4.19 mm / 0.165 in.
Important dates: Premiums for grade rarity, in grades MS-69 and MS-70.

AMERICAN SILVER EAGLE $1 (1986 TO DATE)

Shown actual size
(40.1 mm / 1.58 in.)

Obverse: Walking Liberty, by Adolph Weinman.
Reverse: Heraldic eagle, from the Seal of the President of the United States, by John Mercanti.
Edge: Reeded.
Mintmarks: P, W, S, on reverse, lower left, under the olive branch.
Metallic content: 99.9% silver, 0.1% copper.

Weight: 31.1 grams / 1.09 oz.
Actual silver weight: 31.1 grams / 1 oz.
Important dates: 1995-W; 2008-W, Burnished, Reverse of 2007.
Note: Premiums for grade rarity, for grades MS-69, MS-70, Proof-69, and Proof-70.

GOLD BULLION
AMERICAN GOLD EAGLE BULLION (1986 TO DATE)

$5, tenth-ounce, shown actual size (16.5 mm / 0.65 in.).

$10, quarter-ounce, shown actual size (22 mm / 0.87 in.).

$25, half-ounce, shown actual size (27 mm / 1.07 in.).

$50, one-ounce, shown actual size (32.7 mm / 1.29 in.).

GOLD BULLION

Obverse: Striding Liberty, by Augustus Saint-Gaudens.
Reverse: Family of eagles, by Miley Busiek.
Edge: Reeded.
Mintmarks: P, W, S, on obverse, below the date. There are no mintmarks on bullion versions sold in the investor market.
Metallic content: 91.67% gold, 5.33% copper, 3% silver.

Weights: ($5) 3.39 grams / 0.11 oz. ($10) 8.48 grams / 0.27 oz. ($25) 16.97 grams / 0.55 oz. ($50) 33.93 grams / 1.09 oz.
Actual gold weights: ($5) 0.10 oz. ($10) 0.25 oz. ($25) 0.50 oz. ($50) 1.00 oz.
Note: Premiums are paid for grade rarity, particularly MS-69, MS-70, Proof-69, and Proof-70.

AMERICAN BUFFALO GOLD BULLION (2006 TO DATE)

$5, tenth-ounce, shown actual size (16.5 mm / 0.65 in.).

$10, quarter-ounce, shown actual size (22 mm / 0.87 in.).

$25, half-ounce, shown actual size (27 mm / 1.07 in.).

$50, one-ounce, shown actual size (32.7 mm / 1.29 in.).

Obverse: Indian Head, by James Earle Fraser.
Reverse: American bison, by James Earle Fraser.
Edge: Reeded.
Mintmark: W, on collector coins, on obverse, left of the Indian's neck, below the feathers; no mintmarks on bullion versions sold in the investor market.
Metallic content: 99.99% gold.

Weights: ($5) 3.11 grams / 0.10 oz. ($10) 7.78 grams / 0.25 oz. ($25) 15.55 grams / 0.50 oz.; ($50) 31.10 grams / 1.00 oz.
Actual gold weights: ($5) 0.10 oz. ($10) 0.25 oz. ($25) 0.50 oz. ($50) 1.00 oz.
Note: Premiums paid for grade rarity, particularly MS-69, MS-70, Proof-69, and Proof-70.

FIRST SPOUSE $10 GOLD BULLION (2007–2016)

Actual size:
26.49 mm / 1.043 in.

Obverses: Portraits of first ladies of the United States, by various artists. Issued at the rate of four per year, in conjunction with the Presidential dollar coins. In cases where a president served without a spouse, the obverse design is emblematic of Liberty, as depicted on a circulating coin issued during his term of office.
Reverses: Designs by various artists, featuring images emblematic of the life and work of the first lady depicted on the obverse. In cases where a president served without a spouse, the reverse design is emblematic of a theme from the president's life.
Edge: Reeded.
Mintmark: W, on obverse, below the date.
Metallic content: 99.99% gold.
Weight: 0.5 oz.
Actual gold weight: 0.5 oz.
Note: Premiums paid for grade rarity, particularly MS-69, MS-70, Proof-69, and Proof-70.

See the following pages for illustrations of all First Spouse gold bullion issued to date.

GOLD BULLION

2007, Martha Washington.

2007, Abigail Adams.

2007, Thomas Jefferson's Liberty.

2007, Dolley Madison.

2008, Elizabeth Monroe.

2008, Louisa Adams.

2008, Andrew Jackson's Liberty.

2008, Martin Van Buren's Liberty.

2009, Anna Harrison.

2009, Letitia Tyler.   2009, Julia Tyler.

2009, Sarah Polk.   2009, Margaret Taylor.

2010, Abigail Fillmore.   2010, Jane Pierce.

2010, James Buchanan's Liberty.

2010, Mary Lincoln.

2011, Eliza Johnson.

2011, Julia Grant.

2011, Lucy Hayes.

2011, Lucretia Garfield.

2012, Alice Paul.

2012, Frances Cleveland, variety 1.

2012, Caroline Harrison.   2012, Frances Cleveland, variety 2.

2013, Ida McKinley.

2013, Edith Roosevelt.   2013, Helen Taft.

2013, Ellen Wilson.   2013, Edith Wilson.

2014, Florence Harding.   2014, Grace Coolidge.

2014, Lou Hoover.   2014, Eleanor Roosevelt

MMIX ULTRA HIGH RELIEF $20 GOLD BULLION (2009)

Actual size:
27 mm / 1.07 in.

Photographed at an angle
to show the lettered edge
and the depth of relief.

Obverse: Striding Liberty, by Augustus Saint-Gaudens.
Reverse: Eagle in flight, by Augustus Saint-Gaudens.
Edge: E PLURIBUS UNUM with a star separating each letter.
Mintmark: None (all struck at the Philadelphia Mint).

Metallic content: 99.99% gold.
Weight: 31.1 grams / 1 oz.
Actual gold weight: 1 oz.
Note: Premiums paid for grade rarity, particularly MS-69, MS-70, Proof-69, and Proof-70.

PLATINUM BULLION
AMERICAN PLATINUM EAGLE BULLION (1997 TO DATE)

$10, tenth-ounce, shown actual
size (16.5 mm / 0.65 in.).

$25, quarter-ounce, shown actual size
(22 mm / 0.87 in.).

$50, half-ounce, shown actual size
(27 mm / 1.07 in.).

$100, one-ounce, shown actual size (32.7 mm / 1.29 in.).

Obverse: Statue of Liberty, by John Mercanti.

Reverses: Soaring eagle, by Thomas D. Rogers Sr. The reverses for Proof versions, beginning in 1998, change yearly and are designed by various artists.

Edge: Reeded.

Mintmark: W, on collector coins, on reverse. Positions vary. No mintmarks on bullion versions sold in the investor market.

Metallic content: 100% platinum (.9995 fine).

Weights: ($10) 3.112 grams / 0.1001 oz. ($25) 7.780 grams / 0.2501 oz. ($50) 15.56 grams / 0.5003 oz. ($100) 31.12 grams / 1.0005 oz.

Actual platinum weights: ($10) 0.10 oz. ($25) 0.25 oz. ($50) 0.50 oz. ($100) 1.00 oz.

Note: Premiums paid for grade rarity, particularly MS-69, MS-70, Proof-69, and Proof-70.

1998, Eagle Over New England, Proof reverse.

1999, Eagle Above Southeastern Wetlands, Proof reverse.

2000, Eagle Above America's Heartland, Proof reverse.

2001, Eagle Above America's Southwest, Proof reverse.

2002, Eagle Fishing in America's Northwest, Proof reverse.

2003, Eagle on Rocky Mountain Pine Branch, Proof reverse.

2004, "America" by
Daniel Chester French,
Proof reverse.

2005, Eagle on Heraldic
Shield, Proof reverse.

2006, Legislative Branch,
Proof reverse.

2007, Executive Branch,
Proof reverse.

2008, Judicial Branch,
Proof reverse.

2009, To Form a
More Perfect Union,
Proof reverse.

2010, To Establish
Justice, Proof reverse.

2011, To Insure Domestic
Tranquility, Proof reverse.

2012, To Provide
for the Common
Defence, Proof reverse.

2013, To Promote
the General Welfare,
Proof reverse.

CLASSIC COMMEMORATIVES
(1892–1954)

Obverses: Various motifs honoring important places, people, events, and anniversaries.

Reverses: Various designs corresponding to the places, people, events, and anniversaries honored on the obverse.

Edge: Reeded.

Mintmarks: P, D, S, or none, depending on where the coin was minted.

Metallic content: 90% silver or 90% gold alloy, identical to circulating coins of the same denomination and time period.

Weight: Identical to circulating coins of the same denomination and time period.

Actual precious-metal weight: Identical to circulating coins of the same denomination and time period.

Important dates: All are collectible; types range from common to scarce. Gold commemoratives are particularly valuable. Among the silver coins: 1900 Lafayette dollar; 1922 Grant Memorial half dollar, with star in field; 1928 Hawaiian Sesquicentennial half dollar; 1935 Hudson, New York, Sesquicentennial half dollar; 1935 Old Spanish Trail half dollar; 1937 Battle of Antietam Anniversary half dollar.

Actual size:
30.61 mm / 1.21 in.

World's Columbian Exposition half dollar (1892–1893).

Actual size:
24.26 mm / 0.96 in.

World's Columbian Exposition, Isabella quarter (1893).

Lafayette dollar (1900). Shown actual size (38.1 mm / 1.5 in.).

Actual size:
14.86 mm / 0.59 in.

Louisiana Purchase Exposition, Jefferson variety, gold dollar (1903).

Actual size:
14.86 mm / 0.59 in.

Louisiana Purchase Exposition, McKinley variety, gold dollar (1903).

Actual size:
14.86 mm / 0.59 in.

Lewis and Clark Exposition gold dollar (1904–1905).

Actual size:
30.61 mm / 1.21 in.

Panama-Pacific Exposition half dollar (1915).

Actual size:
14.86 mm / 0.59 in.

Panama-Pacific Exposition gold dollar (1915).

Actual size:
18.2 mm / 0.72 in.

Panama-Pacific Exposition quarter eagle (1915).

Panama-Pacific Exposition gold $50, round (1915).
Shown actual size (44 mm / 1.73 in.).

Panama-Pacific Exposition gold $50, octagonal (1915).
Shown actual size (44 mm / 1.73 in.).

Actual size:
14.86 mm / 0.59 in.

McKinley Memorial gold dollar (1916–1917).

Actual size:
30.61 mm / 1.21 in.

Illinois Centennial half dollar (1918).

Actual size:
30.61 mm / 1.21 in.

Maine Centennial half dollar (1920).

Actual size:
30.61 mm / 1.21 in.

Pilgrim Tercentenary half dollar (1920–1921).

Actual size:
30.61 mm / 1.21 in.

Missouri Centennial half dollar (1921).

Actual size:
30.61 mm / 1.21 in.

Alabama Centennial half dollar (1921).

Actual size:
30.61 mm / 1.21 in.

Grant Memorial half dollar (1922).

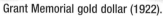

Actual size:
14.86 mm / 0.59 in.

Grant Memorial gold dollar (1922).

Actual size:
30.61 mm / 1.21 in.

Monroe Doctrine Centennial half dollar (1923).

Actual size:
30.61 mm / 1.21 in.

Huguenot-Walloon Tercentenary half dollar (1924).

Actual size:
30.61 mm / 1.21 in.

Lexington-Concord Sesquicentennial half dollar (1925).

Actual size:
30.61 mm / 1.21 in.

Stone Mountain half dollar (1925).

Actual size:
30.61 mm / 1.21 in.

California Diamond Jubilee half dollar (1925).

Actual size:
30.61 mm / 1.21 in.

Fort Vancouver Centennial half dollar (1925).

Actual size:
30.61 mm / 1.21 in.

Sesquicentennial of American Independence half dollar (1926).

Actual size:
18.2 mm / 0.72 in.

Sesquicentennial of American Independence quarter eagle (1926).

Actual size:
30.61 mm / 1.21 in.

Oregon Trail Memorial half dollar (1926–1939).

COMMEMS

Actual size:
30.61 mm / 1.21 in.

Vermont Sesquicentennial half dollar (1927).

Actual size:
30.61 mm / 1.21 in.

Hawaiian Sesquicentennial half dollar (1928).

Actual size:
30.61 mm / 1.21 in.

Maryland Tercentenary half dollar (1934).

Actual size:
30.61 mm / 1.21 in.

Texas Independence Centennial half dollar (1934–1938).

Actual size:
30.61 mm / 1.21 in.

Daniel Boone Bicentennial half dollar (1934–1938).

Actual size:
30.61 mm / 1.21 in.

Connecticut Tercentenary half dollar (1935).

Actual size:
30.61 mm / 1.21 in.

Arkansas Centennial half dollar (1935–1939).

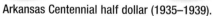

Actual size:
30.61 mm / 1.21 in.

Arkansas Centennial, Robinson reverse, half dollar (1936).

COMMEMS

Actual size:
30.61 mm / 1.21 in.

Hudson, New York, Sesquicentennial half dollar (1936).

Actual size:
30.61 mm / 1.21 in.

California Pacific International Exposition half dollar (1935–1936).

Actual size:
30.61 mm / 1.21 in.

Old Spanish Trail half dollar (1935).

Actual size:
30.61 mm / 1.21 in.

Providence, Rhode Island, Tercentenary half dollar (1936).

Actual size:
30.61 mm / 1.21 in.

Cleveland Centennial / Great Lakes Exposition half dollar (1936).

Actual size:
30.61 mm / 1.21 in.

Wisconsin Territorial Centennial half dollar (1936).

Actual size:
30.61 mm / 1.21 in.

Cincinnati Music Center half dollar (1936).

Actual size:
30.61 mm / 1.21 in.

Long Island Tercentenary half dollar (1936).

COMMEMS

Actual size:
30.61 mm / 1.21 in.

York County, Maine, Tercentenary half dollar (1936).

Actual size:
30.61 mm / 1.21 in.

Bridgeport, Connecticut, Centennial half dollar (1936).

Actual size:
30.61 mm / 1.21 in.

Lynchburg, Virginia, Sesquicentennial half dollar (1936).

Actual size:
30.61 mm / 1.21 in.

Elgin, Illiniois, Centennial half dollar (1936).

Actual size:
30.61 mm / 1.21 in.

Albany, New York, Charter half dollar (1936).

Actual size:
30.61 mm / 1.21 in.

San Francisco – Oakland Bay Bridge Opening half dollar (1936).

Actual size:
30.61 mm / 1.21 in.

Columbia, South Carolina, Sesquicentennial half dollar (1936).

Actual size:
30.61 mm / 1.21 in.

Delaware Tercentenary half dollar (1936).

COMMEMS

Actual size:
30.61 mm / 1.21 in.

Battle of Gettysburg Anniversary half dollar (1936).

Actual size:
30.61 mm / 1.21 in.

Norfolk, Virginia, Bicentennial half dollar (1936).

Actual size:
30.61 mm / 1.21 in.

Roanoke Island, North Carolina, 350th Anniversary half dollar (1937).

Actual size:
30.61 mm / 1.21 in.

Battle of Antietam Anniversary half dollar (1937).

Actual size:
30.61 mm / 1.21 in.

New Rochelle, New York, 250th Anniversary half dollar (1938).

Actual size:
30.61 mm / 1.21 in.

Iowa Centennial half dollar (1946).

Actual size:
30.61 mm / 1.21 in.

Booker T. Washington Memorial half dollar (1946–1951).

Actual size:
30.61 mm / 1.21 in.

Carver/Washington Commemorative half dollar (1951–1954).

COMMEMS

MODERN COMMEMORATIVES (1982 TO DATE)

Obverses: Various motifs honoring important places, people, events, and anniversaries.

Reverses: Various designs corresponding to the places, people, events, and anniversaries honored on the obverse.

Edge: Reeded.

Mintmarks: P, D, S, W, or none, depending on where the coin was minted.

Metallic content: Copper-nickel; 90% silver; or 90% gold; identical to circulating coins of the same denomination.

Weight: Identical to circulating coins of the same denomination. Actual precious-metal weight: Identical to circulating coins of the same denomination.

Important dates: All are collectible; many modern issues are common.

Note: The U.S. Mint has issued more than 100 different commemorative coins since 1982, in half dollar, silver dollar, $5, and $10 denominations. Many modern commemoratives were issued in multiple-coin sets as well as individually. Some commemorative coins were included in special Proof sets, and some have been packaged with medals, intaglio prints, postage stamps, and other collectibles. Modern U.S. Mint packaging includes a certificate of authenticity, and often a special presentation box and slipcase.

LIST OF MODERN COMMEMORATIVES (1982–2014)

Washington's Birth 250th Anniversary (1982)

Los Angeles Olympiad (1983–1984)

Statue of Liberty Centennial (1986)

U.S. Constitution Bicentennial (1987)

Seoul Olympiad (1988)

U.S. Congress Bicentennial (1989)

Eisenhower Centennial (1990)

Mount Rushmore Golden Anniversary (191)

Korean War Memorial (1991)

United Service Organizations (1991)

XXV Olympiad (1992)

White House Bicentennial (1992)

Christopher Columbus Quincentenary (1992)

Bill of Rights (1993)

50th Anniversary of World War II (1991–1995)

World Cup Tournament (1994)

Thomas Jefferson (1993 [1994])

Women in Military Service Memorial (1994)

Vietnam Veterans Memorial (1994)

U.S. Prisoner of War Museum (1994)

U.S. Capitol Bicentennial (1994)

Civil War Battlefield Preservation (1995)

Special Olympics World Games (1995)

XXVI Olympiad (1995–1996)

National Community Service (1996)

Smithsonian Institution 150th Anniversary (1996)

U.S. Botanic Garden (1997)

Franklin D. Roosevelt (1997)

National Law Enforcement Officers Memorial (1997)

Jackie Robinson (1997)

Black Revolutionary War Patriots (1998)

Robert F. Kennedy (1998)

George Washington (1999)

Yellowstone National Park (1999)

Dolley Madison (1999)

Library of Congress Bicentennial (2000)

Leif Ericson Millennium (2001)

U.S. Capitol Visitor Center (2001)

West Point Bicentennial (2002)

Salt Lake City Olympic Games (2002)

First Flight Centennial (2003)

Lewis and Clark Bicentennial (2004)

Thomas Alva Edison (2004)

Chief Justice John Marshall (2005)

Marine Corps 230th Anniversary (2005)

Benjamin Franklin Tercentenary (2006)

San Francisco Old Mint Centennial (2006)

Jamestown 400th Anniversary (2007)

Little Rock Central High School Desegregation (2007)

Bald Eagle (2008)

Abraham Lincoln Bicentennial (2009)

Louise Braille Bicentennial (2009)

American Veterans Disabled for Life (2010)

Boy Scouts of America Centennial (2010)

U.S. Army (2011)

Medal of Honor (2011)

Infantry Soldier (2012)

Star-Spangled Banner (2012)

Girl Scouts of the U.S.A. Centennial (2013)

5-Star Generals (2013)

National Baseball Hall of Fame (2014)

Civil Rights Act of 1964 (2014)

Popularly collected and frequently encountered, Uncirculated and Proof sets seem to be the "ugly ducklings" of the coin market. Turn them into respectable swans.

6

UNCIRCULATED AND PROOF SETS

If you have a stash of coins or have inherited coins from someone who was at least a casual collector anytime from the mid-1950s through the early 2000s, you probably have on hand some Uncirculated sets and some Proof sets produced by the U.S. Mint. They are the Mint's most popular and longest continually offered products.

UNCIRCULATED SETS

Uncirculated sets, sometimes referred to as "Mint sets," contain examples from each mint facility that produced coins for circulation in a given year. For most years since 1947 (when the U.S. Mint began selling Uncirculated sets), the coins contained within them have been circulation strikes that were packaged and sold to collectors who wanted a complete date-and-mintmark set for the year, free of circulation wear. In 2000, in order to eliminate some of the marks that circulation-strike coins naturally receive in the manufacturing and storage process, the Mint began to use a "satin finish" on coins in its Uncirculated sets. This continued through 2010. In 2011 the Mint upgraded to a "brilliant finish."

The Mint did not sell Uncirculated sets in 1982 and 1983, as it was changing alloys in the Lincoln cent. Thus Souvenir Sets, sold in the gift shops at the Denver and Philadelphia minting facilities, became the primary sources of Uncirculated coins for those two years.

One of the most sought-after Uncirculated sets is dated 1996. It contains all of the denominations struck for circulation at the Denver and Philadelphia mints. However, it also contains a Roosevelt dime bearing a W mintmark for the West Point Mint. The coin commemorates the 50th anniversary of the Roosevelt dime and it was available only in the 1996 Uncirculated set. If you have the 1996 Uncirculated set, be sure to set it aside. The 1996-W Roosevelt dime in high grades (MS-67 and higher) is worth more than the going price for the set. If your coin has pristine surfaces, it would be a serious candidate to remove from the set to be professionally graded and sold as an individual coin.

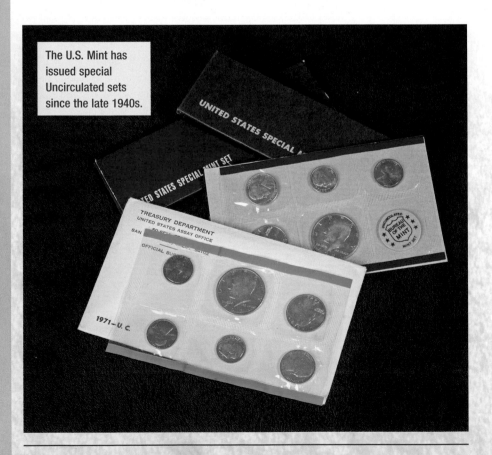

The U.S. Mint has issued special Uncirculated sets since the late 1940s.

Earlier Uncirculated sets, too, are worth special note because they contain coins that were only available in the sets. The 1970-D Kennedy half dollar was available only in the 1970 Uncirculated set. The 1973-P and 1973-D Eisenhower dollars were available only in the 1973 Uncirculated set. Individual 40 percent silver Uncirculated Eisenhower dollars, struck at the San Francisco Mint, were sold separately from 1971 through 1974 and are referred to as "Blue Ikes" because they were packaged in cellophane along with a blue plastic token and housed in a blue envelope.

Uncirculated sets produced in the last decade contain half dollars and dollar coins that are no longer issued for circulation. For example, the Kennedy half dollar has not been produced for circulation since before 2002, but examples are included in the Uncirculated sets. (Each year the U.S. Mint also sells 40-coin rolls and 200-coin bags of new Kennedy half dollars struck at both the Denver and Philadelphia mints, thus the Uncirculated sets are not the only source.) A similar situation exists for the manganese-brass small-dollar coins. The Sacagawea dollar coin, introduced in 2000, was not produced for circulation from 2002 through 2008, but was sold to collectors via Uncirculated sets, rolls, bags, and

So-called Blue Ikes (Uncirculated silver Eisenhower dollars in blue packaging) were sold by the Mint in the early 1970s.

boxes containing large numbers of the coins. Due to their lack of circulation, the secretary of the Treasury halted production of circulation strikes of the Native American and Presidential dollar coins in December of 2011. However, both series continue to be sold directly to collectors in Uncirculated sets, rolls, bags, and boxes.

The highest values for Uncirculated examples of modern U.S. coins are due to *grade rarity*. If you are seeking to obtain the top price for coins in Uncirculated sets, examine your sets closely to find pristine specimens and consider submitting them for grading and certification by one of the top professional coin-grading services. Check the value columns in an advanced price guide (like the Professional Edition Red Book) for MS-68, MS-69, and MS-70 for coins in your sets. Coin dealers and avid collectors make money on Uncirculated sets by breaking up a set and selling its coins individually. So can you, if you have the time and inclination to become involved at this level.

If you elect to sell your Uncirculated sets intact, be sure to keep them in their original packaging. The certificate of authenticity, which the U.S. Mint encloses with each set, is important and should be kept with the set.

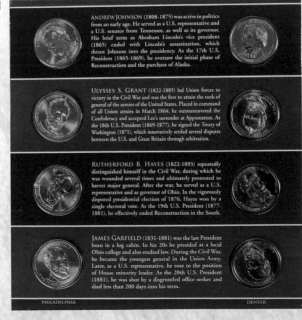

Recent Uncirculated sets include many different modern U.S. coins.

Proof Sets

Proof coins as we know them today descend from a practical application in the early years of the U.S. Mint—striking samples to assure there were no defects in the coinage dies. Today Proof coins are a popular product made especially for the collector market.

Based on Mint records, it is clear that Mint workers had stopped striking coins for "proofing" purposes by 1816. It is equally clear (from surviving coins) that by 1836 the Mint began to strike Proof coins that were given special attention in manufacturing, to provide as presentation gifts and as examples of the minter's art. Proof coins from 1836 through 1842 could be purchased individually, by denomination, directly from the Mint. Buying Proof coins as complete sets (that included an example of each denomination struck for circulation during the year) came into vogue in 1850. For the remainder of the 19th century and even in the early decades of the 20th century Proof coins—if they were struck in a given year—tended to have mintages in the hundreds or single-digit thousands due to the relatively small number of coin collectors in the United States who were interested in buying them.

Fort Worth, Texas, coin dealer B. Max Mehl popularized coin collecting beginning in 1924 when he used magazine and newspaper advertising to sell his stock of coins. But more importantly, Mehl launched the American public on quests to find particular coins, for which he offered huge premiums. As attention to coin collecting grew, the U.S Mint again began to sell coins directly to collectors. From 1936 to 1942 it sold sets with Proof versions of the five denominations in circulation. (It also offered a six-coin set in 1942 that included the silver wartime five-cent coin.) The Mint suspended Proof coin production in 1943 and did not resume until 1950, when it sold an astounding 51,386 sets—more than double the number it had sold in 1942.

As more information became available about coin collecting through hobby monthly magazines and weekly newspapers, the hobby began to explode in numbers. In 1956 the Mint sold 669,384 Proof sets. In 1957 it sold 1,247,952 sets! The modern Proof set had come into its own, with millions of sets being sold annually becoming the norm.

Packaging began to change as sales grew. Coins in Proof sets from 1950 to 1955 were sealed individually in cellophane bags before being packaged in a box. "Flat packs" containing coins sealed in cellophane and enclosed in an envelope were introduced in 1955 and continued through 1964.

From the 1930s until the mid-1950s, collectors could order Proof coins individually or in sets. "If you had placed your order for a Proof set early in 1955," writes David W. Lange in the *Guide Book of Modern United States Proof Coin Sets,* "your coins would have been delivered in individual envelopes stapled together and wrapped in tissue paper for protection, then sealed inside a small cardboard box with postal tape. . . ." Midway through that year, the Mint started using a single "pliofilm" envelope with individually sealed compartments for each coin.

Collector interest in Proof sets exploded in the late 1950s.

Proof set production was suspended from 1965 through 1967, as the nation abandoned the silver standard for its subsidiary coinage (dimes, quarters, and half dollars) and changed to the copper-nickel alloy. The Mint offered Special Mint Sets during these three years. The Special Mint Sets containing circulation strikes of the denominations in circulation were produced at the San Francisco Assay Office for sale to collectors, but none of the coins bear a mintmark.

When Proof set production resumed in 1968, the Mint introduced new packaging: hard plastic holders. It has continued to offer Proof sets since then, with varying numbers of coins reflective of the particular year's denominations, in plastic holders. The nation's bicentennial year, 1976, brought the zenith of Proof sets, with 4,149,730 sets sold.

Until the mid-20th century, Proof coins were primarily distinguishable by their high-quality surfaces. But gradually over the past five decades the Mint has positioned its Proof coins as its top-of-the-line

The Bicentennial quarter, half dollar, and dollar were issued in copper-nickel in 1975 and 1976 Proof sets, and also in silver for a special three-coin Proof set (pictured).

products. Modern Proof coins are struck on highly polished planchets and from dies that have been specially polished and treated to produce mirror-like surfaces and frosting on the raised portions of the designs. Typically modern Proof coins are struck at least twice in order to force the metal into all the crevices of the die, resulting in very fine detail on the coin.

The U.S. Mint has also issued special Proof sets over the years. One of the most popular, and frequently encountered in coins passed on to family members, is the special 1976 Proof set containing three 40 percent silver clad coins. The quarter, half dollar, and dollar coins in the set contain special reverses honoring the Bicentennial of the United States. Other frequently found Proof coins are what collectors refer to as the "Brown Ikes." The name derives from the brown slipcase-box outer packaging for the plastic case housing Proof versions of the 40 percent silver clad Eisenhower dollars from 1971 through 1974.

In 1983 the Mint launched an expanded set, dubbed the "Prestige Proof Set." These were sold from 1983 to 1997, except for 1985. In addition to the year's regular Proof coins, the Prestige Proof set contained

"Brown Ikes"—Proof silver Eisenhower dollars packaged in brown slipcase boxes—were issued by the Mint from 1971 through 1974.

Proof examples of commemorative coins struck that year, usually of the dollar denomination. The product was renamed the "Legacy Proof Set" in 2005 and continued yearly through 2008.

Due to the draw-down of the Treasury's 1979–1980 stockpile of Susan B. Anthony dollars, in 1999 the Mint had to produce new Anthony dollars for use in commerce. Proof sets for 1999 had already been struck and were on sale when Anthony dollar production began. Proof versions of the 1999 Anthony dollar were sold separately in a blue velvet presentation box near the end of the year.

Among the most popular of the U.S. Mint's most recent special sets containing Proof coins is the "Coins & Chronicles Set" that was produced in 2009 to honor the bicentennial of Abraham Lincoln's birth and the centennial of the Lincoln cent series. The set includes Proof versions of the four 2009 Lincoln cents (featuring special reverses highlighting significant milestones in Lincoln's life), plus the Proof version of the Lincoln commemorative silver dollar issued in 2009.

Prestige Proof sets, issued by the Mint from 1983 through 1997, featured the year's regular Proof coins as well as any commemoratives minted that year.

Silver Proof Sets

With an eye toward helping sell the silver in the U.S. government's Strategic and Critical Materials Stockpile, Congress approved in 1990 (and President George H.W. Bush signed into law on November 15, 1990) the Silver Coin Proof Sets Act (Public Law 101-585). This authorized the U.S. Mint to strike Proof versions of three of the current coins struck for circulation (the dime, quarter, and half dollar) in 90 percent silver and 10 percent copper. (Once the silver stockpile was depleted, the law authorized the secretary of the Treasury to purchase U.S.–mined silver at prevailing world market prices in order to continue striking the sets.)

The Mint launched its new Silver Proof set product in 1992, combining the three 90 percent silver coins with the Proof versions of the year's Lincoln cent and Jefferson five-cent coins struck in their standard compositions. The Mint continued offering the five coins in the Silver Proof set through 1998. During these early years the Mint offered two packaging versions. The standard option offered the silver set in a plastic case enclosed in a black box to distinguish it from the purple packaging used for the copper-nickel clad Proof set containing the same five denominations.

Silver versions of the dime, quarter, and half dollar are included in the Silver Proof sets that the U.S. Mint debuted in 1992.

The Silver Proof set was also offered in what the Mint dubbed its Premier Silver Proof set. The coins were enclosed in a plastic case that was housed within a black-velvet and white-satin presentation case. The certificate of authenticity was printed on parchment paper rather than the standard white paper used for other certificates. The more expensive Premier Silver Proof set was aimed at the gift-giving market. Coins in both sets carried the S mintmark, signifying San Francisco as the minting facility.

When first introduced, the Silver Proof set seemed to be an instant hit, with sales in 1992 reaching 1,009,586 for the regular Silver Proof set and 308,055 for the Premier Silver Proof set. The regular Silver Proof set settled in above the two-million mark for several years, but hit a low in 1995, with only 549,878 sold. The low mintage led to secondary-market demand and premiums for the lower-mintage sets. With the rise in precious-metal prices in the early years of the 21st century, the Silver Proof set once again became popular.

The startup of the 50 State Quarters® Program in 1999 expanded the number of coins in both the traditional clad Proof set as well as the Silver Proof set, with five quarters included rather than one. Perhaps due to the cost and sheer number of coins offered, sales of the nine-coin Silver Proof set in 1999 turned out to be the lowest of the 10-year program. It thus became the key to the Silver Proof sets including State quarters. The Mint included silver quarters in the Silver Proof sets for the 2009 D.C. and Territories program as well as the America the Beautiful quarter series that launched in 2010.

The earlier Silver Proof sets (1992 through 1998) including three 90 percent silver coins contain a total of 0.180845 troy ounces of silver. Silver Proof sets containing the five State quarters plus the dime and half dollar (1999 through 2008) contain 1.33823 troy ounces of silver. In 2009, the Silver Proof set contained six quarters (for the D.C. and Territories program) plus the dime and half dollar, with a total of 1.51907 troy ounces of silver. Beginning in 2010, with production of five America the Beautiful quarters, the Silver Proof set returned to a total of 1.33823 troy ounces of silver.

Important Proof Dates

Due to low mintages and continuing demand, all Proof sets from 1936 through 1942 and from 1950 through 1955 carry significant premiums. Among the most valuable Proof sets produced since 1968 are those that contain error coins. Significant dates to check:

1968-S Proof set (Roosevelt dime without mintmark)

1970-S Proof set (Roosevelt dime without mintmark)

1971-S Proof set (Jefferson nickel without mintmark)

1975-S Proof set (Roosevelt dime without mintmark)

1983-S Prestige Proof set (Roosevelt dime without mintmark)

1990-S Proof set and Prestige Proof set (Lincoln cent without mintmark)

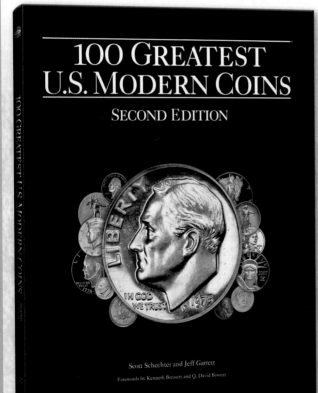

The cover of *100 Greatest U.S. Modern Coins,* second edition, featured the famous and ultra-rare (only two known) 1975 Proof dime without the normal S mintmark.

Only two of the 1975-S Proof sets have been found with the Roosevelt dime missing its S mintmark. The dime from one of the sets was graded Proof-68 by Professional Coin Grading Service and sold at public auction August 18, 2011, for $349,600.

Proof sets are among the U.S. Mint's most popular collectibles, with annual sales reaching into the millions.

An overview of U.S. paper money types printed since 1861 in the order they were authorized by Congress, with images of the most frequently encountered types.

7

IDENTIFYING PAPER MONEY BY DESIGN TYPE

From the founding of the republic until the Civil War, all federal currency in the United States was coined in copper, silver, or gold. By early 1861 it was evident that additional money would be needed to deal with the impending national crisis. Just three months after the first shots were fired at Fort Sumter, South Carolina, on April 12, 1861, the federal government was in need of money in coined form to purchase needed equipment for its troops. On July 17, 1861, Congress authorized the secretary of the Treasury to issue paper money, known as Demand Notes because they were to be payable in gold coins upon demand. The Demand Notes, issued in the same year they were authorized, are considered the first U.S. federal paper money. They were essentially government IOUs. The notes were printed by private printers under contract with the federal government. Demand Notes became known as *greenbacks* because green ink was used on the back side and black ink was used on the face or front side of the notes.

By February 1862 it was evident the government did not have enough gold to redeem all of the notes that had been printed, so Congress authorized a new classification of paper money. Legal Tender Notes were to be printed by private firms under contract beginning in April. Soon after, Treasury officials began to acquire presses and other equipment to overprint seals and trim the notes. They also sought permission for the Treasury Department to engrave and print notes, thus creating the pathway for what would become the Bureau of Engraving and Printing (the BEP)— the nation's paper-money–producing factory.

The public began to hoard coins shortly after the Civil War began. U.S. silver coins during the war were also exported for profit due to high silver prices being paid abroad. The federal government responded in 1862 by issuing Fractional Currency—paper notes in denominations of less than a dollar. The first issues were called Postage Currency because they resembled postage stamps. Later Fractional Notes looked more like federal Legal Tender Notes, although they were smaller in size.

A $5 Demand Note, Series of 1861—one of the first federal "greenbacks."

As the Civil War progressed, the federal government needed more money. In 1863 Congress approved the National Banking Act, which attempted to regulate private banks and the nation's chaotic currency

A $5 Legal Tender Note from the Series of 1862.

Postage Currency of 1862—note the U.S. POSTAGE / TEN CENTS engraving on the face.

system. At the time, the United States did not have a central bank. The new law encouraged private banks to become national banks through a federal chartering process. Once chartered they could use their funds to purchase Union bonds, deposit the bonds with the U.S. Treasury, and then issue National Bank Notes for up to 90 percent of the value of the Union bonds on deposit. The net result was the creation of more money that the federal government could tap for the war effort. In 1863, 179 private banks became national banks. By the end of the war in 1865 there were nearly 2,000 national banks. (When the last National Bank Notes were printed in 1935, there were more than 14,000 national banks, each with the authority to issue legal-tender paper money with its name on it.)

Federal paper money was born of necessity, but even after the Civil War paper notes of various types and denominations continued to be issued as the nation expanded and encountered twists and turns in its economic development.

The types of federal paper money issued include Demand Notes, Fractional Currency, large and small-size Legal Tender Notes (also known as United States Notes), Compound Interest Treasury Notes, Interest Bearing Notes, Refunding Certificates, large- and small-size Silver Certificates, Treasury (Coin) Notes, large- and small-size National Bank Notes, Federal Reserve Bank Notes, Gold Certificates, and Federal Reserve Notes.

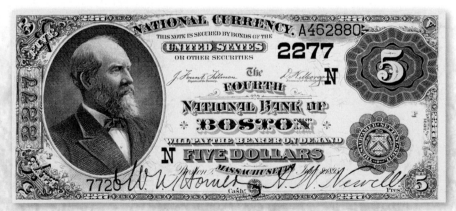

A $5 National Bank Note issued by the Fourth National Bank of Boston, Series of 1882.

Note the reference to *large-size* and *small-size* notes. Federal paper money in denominations of $1 and greater issued prior to 1929 are known as large-size notes because they are 25 percent larger than the smaller-size notes in circulation today. Large-size notes in circulation before 1929 measure 3.125 inches by 7.4218 inches. Small-size notes measure 2.61 inches by 6.14 inches (with a thickness of 0.0043 inches). The reduction in size was primarily to save costs in printing the notes, but the Treasury Department also used the changeover to bring more uniformity to U.S. paper money.

IDENTIFYING SMALL-SIZE NOTES

Most coin collections and accumulations inherited today or passed down to younger generations tend to also have one or a few pieces of small-size currency. So our focus is to assist in identifying the various types of small-size notes. They include:

Currency Type	Issue Dates	Seal Color	Denominations
Legal Tender Notes	1928, 1966	Red	$1, $2, $5, $100 ($1 in Series 1928; $100 in Series 1966)
Gold Certificates	1928–1933	Gold	$10, $20, $50, $100, $500, $1,000, $5,000, $10,000
National Bank Notes	1929–1935	Brown	$5, $10, $20, $50, $100
Federal Reserve Bank Notes	1929	Brown	$5, $10, $20, $50, $100
Silver Certificates	1928–1963	Blue	$1, $5, $10
Federal Reserve Notes	1928 to date	Green	$1, $2, $5, $10, $20, $50, $100, $500, $1,000, $5,000, $10,000

Not all denominations were issued in each series, but the above chart will help you determined what type of small-size note you may have. Paper money is collected by type, series, signature combinations, as well as by designs. Grade or condition of the note is supremely important.

If you have either large-size or small-size U.S. paper money that appears to be in pristine condition (without folds, creases, or marks), it is highly recommend that you obtain a value guide with images of each type that also contains pricing information by grade. One of the best and most economical sources is *A Guide Book of United States Paper Money*, by Arthur L. and Ira S. Friedberg.

WORLD WAR II NOTES

There is one special kind of federal paper money that seems to show up frequently in collections handed down through families. They are special notes used during World War II and likely were brought home by those who served in the military during the war.

The Japanese attack on Pearl Harbor, December 7, 1941, brought into focus the possibility of a larger Japanese invasion. To lessen the likelihood of U.S. paper money falling into enemy hands, the BEP printed special notes that could be instantly declared worthless or demonetized. The notes printed for special use were $1 Silver Certificates and Federal Reserve Notes in the denominations of $5, $10, and $20. All of the notes have brown seals and brown serial numbers. The word HAWAII is printed on each end of the face and HAWAII is overprinted in large letters on the back. From August 15, 1942, until October 22, 1944, no other paper money could be used in the Hawaiian Islands without a special license.

In a similar vein, Silver Crtificates were printed in 1942 for use during invasions in North Africa and Italy. They have yellow seals and the serial numbers are printed in blue.

STAR NOTES

If the BEP deems a printed note to be defective during the inspection process, it replaces the note (or, typically, the entire pack the note would

The $10 Federal Reserve Note, Series of 1934-A, with HAWAII overprinted at the left and right ends on the face, and with a large HAWAII overprint on the back.

A famous World War II note: the $5 Silver Certificate, Series of 1934-A, with a distinctive yellow Treasury seal and serial numbers printed in blue.

have been part of) with prepared-in-advance substitute notes, whose replacement status is indicated by a star. On Federal Reserve Notes the star is placed after the serial number; on all other types the star appears before the serial number. Since the BEP's numbering machines have only eight digits, a star is also used when the 100 millionth note in a series is printed.

The use of stars did not begin until 1910. Thus stars on paper money before 1910 are part of the design and do not identify the note as a replacement note.

A $5 Treasury Note of 1891; the star following the serial number is ornamental only.

A $2 Federal Reserve Note with a star following the serial number.

ERROR NOTES

Errors of varying kinds have escaped the BEP inspection process. They range from the dramatic—e.g., the face or back missing seals, serial numbers, or other major design elements—to the barely noticeable. Error notes are avidly collected. Inspect any paper money, old or new, to make sure all of the design elements are in the correct places and the various colors of ink are correct for the type of note. Images of error types and values for the known types by series and denominations are listed in most paper-money value guides.

A $20 Federal Reserve Note with the back design showing on the face.

A $1 Federal Reserve Note printed in error, with the second printing (the main front design) missing.

UE · AND · VA

WASHINGTON

N. L.

It may be round and shiny, but that does not make it a U.S. coin. Tips for identifying tokens, medals, and other money substitutes as well as foreign coins, and how to locate information on their values.

8

IF IT'S NOT A U.S. COIN . . .

Many people make the mistake of calling "coins" all items that are round and shiny and near in size to coins. As noted in chapter 3, coins have a legal definition. They are authorized and issued by a government for use as money. A coin features a design device authorized by the issuing government and usually states its value or denomination. Most coins are round, but they can be of different shapes and sizes.

A simple test is helpful in identifying a U.S. coin. Unless the answer is yes to these three questions, it is not a U.S. coin:

1. Does it bear a date?
2. Does it state a denomination, in words and/ or numerals?
3. Does it contain the legends LIBERTY and UNITED STATES OF AMERICA?

Most U.S. coins also contain the motto E PLURI-BUS UNUM. The motto IN GOD WE TRUST first appeared on the two-cent coin in 1864 and was added to other denominations in years following, although its appearance was interrupted on some

These round, metallic objects share a similar theme: the great American pastime, baseball. But only one of them is a *coin*. The silver dollar can be identified as an official U.S. coin by its date (1992), denomination (ONE DOLLAR), and legends (LIBERTY and UNITED STATES OF AMERICA). The other item is actually a *medal*—an 1861 souvenir of the Pioneer Base Ball Club—and not a legal-tender coin. (Both shown enlarged.)

denominations such as the five-cent coin. It was left off the new Liberty Head five-cent series in 1883 and did not reappear on the denomination until 1938, when the first Jefferson five-cent coin was struck. IN GOD WE TRUST has been in continuous use on all gold coins, silver dollars, half dollars, and quarter dollars struck since July 1, 1908. It has appeared on the one-cent denomination since 1909 and has been used continuously on the dime since 1916. All U.S. coins struck since 1938, regardless of denomination or metal content, bear the IN GOD WE TRUST motto. The only exceptions are error coins, such as when some 2007 and 2008 Presidential dollars left the U.S. Mint without the edge lettering that included the mottos.

It is possible to find coin-like objects that are exact replicas of U.S. coins. Telemarketers and infomercials since early 2000 have aggressively sold replicas of various U.S. coins, particularly gold coins, and called them "coins" in advertising. For example: There is only one 1933 Saint-Gaudens double eagle $20 gold coin that has been declared legal to own by the U.S. Treasury. It was sold at public auction for a record $7.59 million in 2002, and shortly afterward the airwaves were saturated with commercials selling a "Proof tribute $20 gold coin." It was an exact replica of the real gold coin—complete with all of the legends and mottos—but it contained very little gold. It was a copper-nickel piece plated with a microscopic layer of the precious metal.

The best clue that such items are not genuine coins is the word COPY, which has been required since 1973 to be incused on all replicas of numismatic items made and/or sold in the United States. Examine suspect items carefully because the marketers are expert at hiding the word COPY within the design devices. It is usually placed on the reverse, but it is sometimes on the obverse.

Since about 2005 Chinese counterfeiters have made and aggressively sold replicas of virtually all U.S. coins. Although many web sites offering them describe the items as "replicas," the failure to comply with U.S. law requiring the word COPY to be incused on each replica makes them *counterfeits*. Many of the Chinese-made counterfeits meet all of the specifications of genuine U.S. coins in metal content, diameter, weight, and specific gravity. Thus it takes a highly knowledgeable collector, dealer, or expert grader/authenticator to spot such counterfeits. If, among the coins you have inherited, there are complete collections by date and mintmark of various denominations in albums, it would be worth trying to find out how long they may have been in the person's possession. If there are any receipts or notes to indicate that the coins may have been purchased online or at local general auctions within the last decade, it would be prudent to arrange to have them tested for authenticity. Professional third-party grading services authenticate coins, and it is possible to submit coins for authentication without requesting that the coins be graded. (See the professional coin-grading service listing in chapter 10 for contact information.) These companies charge a fee for authenticating coins, so inquire about the cost before submitting your coins. If submitting all of the suspect coins in cost prohibitive, select key dates within each series to send in. Since key dates are the most valuable, there is a higher probability of their being counterfeit. It may be advisable to instruct the grading service to grade the key dates if they are determined to be genuine.

This replica of a 1795 $5 gold coin clearly has the word COPY marked on it—as required by U.S. law. (Shown enlarged.)

These may appear to be genuine (and valuable) U.S. coins—but they're actually base-metal counterfeits made in China. Carefully examine your coins against photographs like the ones in chapter 5.

One of these 1885-S Morgan dollars is genuine and the other is counterfeit. Rare and valuable coins should be carefully examined to make sure they're authentic. See the last page of this book to find out which coin is real.

MEDALS AND MEDALLIONS

Most non-coin items called "coins" in modern marketing are actually medals. Two popular types of medals that are often mistakenly called coins are "sports coins" and "challenge coins." These are medals, and not real coins.

Sports coins are usually silver-dollar sized and feature the logos of sports teams or portraits of players in their designs. One sports coin that is seen by millions of people each year is the piece used for the coin-toss prior to beginning of the Super Bowl football game.

Challenge coins trace their origin at least as far back as World War I (1914–1918). They are often silver-dollar sized but are made of bronze and bear an insignia or emblem, usually enameled. In the military, challenge coins are presented by commanders to recognize special achievement by a member of the unit, or to enhance morale. Members of the unit are encouraged to carry the challenge coin at all times and use it to prove membership in the unit, if challenged to do so. In recent decades, use of challenge coins has spread to various executive departments of government to recognize special achievement. Members of social and

Examples of challenge coins (actually *medals*) from the FBI and the Department of State.

civic organizations often use them as mementos of events and to exchange them with fellow attendees. Even the president of the United States has a challenge coin and presents it on occasion. Challenge coins are highly collectible but they are not actually coins that can be used as money.

Millions of medals have been produced in the United States. Most are commemorative in nature and honor people, places, and events. The predominant metal used for medals is bronze, although some are also struck in precious metals such as silver and gold. Many medals are privately issued but some are struck and issued by the federal government via the U.S. Mint. The Mint has struck Indian Peace medals, national medals, presidential medals, and medals authorized and awarded by Congress. Currently the U.S. Mint is striking bronze medallic versions of the gold $10 First Spouse bullion coins. The medals carry the coins' obverse and reverse designs, but do not contain a value or denomination reference.

The U.S. government created special Peace medals—like this one from the Lewis and Clark expedition—for presentation as gifts to leaders of Native American tribes.

Major categories of privately issued medals include those honoring expositions and fairs, political campaign medals, inaugural medals, prize medals, academic medals, institutional medals, heroism and lifesaving medals, and art medals.

Medallion is a term used to describe large medals, usually three inches or greater in diameter. The U.S. Mint struck and issued a series of what it called the American Arts Gold Medallions from 1980 through 1984 in one-ounce and half-ounce sizes. They featured obverse portraits of great American artists, writers, and actors including Grant Wood, Marian Anderson, Mark Twain, Willa Cather, Louis Armstrong, Frank Lloyd Wright, Robert Frost, Alexander Calder, Helen Hayes, and John Steinbeck. Due to an unwieldy ordering process and a lackluster reception in the marketplace, sales numbers were relatively low. The first year of issue, 1980, the medallions were made of 90 percent gold and 10 percent

Many private firms have issued collectible medals in copper, nickel, silver, and many other compositions. Pictured are silver medals from the Franklin Mint's "Spirit of Scouting" collection.

copper. From 1981 through 1984 they were made of 90 percent gold, 7 percent copper, and 3 percent silver. All were struck at the West Point Bullion Depository but they do not bear a mintmark.

American Arts Gold Medallions

Year	Portrait	Size	Sold
1980	Grant Wood	1 oz.	312,709
1980	Marian Anderson	1/2 oz.	281,624
1981	Mark Twain	1 oz.	116,371
1981	Willa Cather	1/2 oz.	97,331
1982	Louis Armstrong	1 oz.	409,098
1982	Frank Lloyd Wright	1/2 oz.	348,305
1983	Robert Frost	1 oz.	390,669
1983	Alexander Calder	1/2 oz.	74,571
1984	Helen Hayes	1 oz.	33,546
1984	John Steinbeck	1/2 oz.	32,572

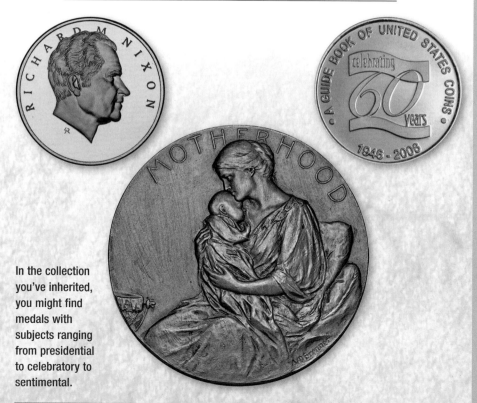

In the collection you've inherited, you might find medals with subjects ranging from presidential to celebratory to sentimental.

There is no way to determine how many of the American Arts Gold Medallions have survived the melting pot as the price for gold has risen. The medallions with the lowest sales numbers appear to bring substantial premiums in the collector market. With gold at $1,300 per ounce, one would reap four to five times the original 1980s purchase price of most.

The American Arts Gold Medallions of the early 1980s were struck by the U.S. Mint, but they aren't coins—they have no legal-tender status.

TOKENS

Many coin-like items are tokens, which are substitutes for money. Many tokens are made of copper or brass, but tokens can be made of any alloy or substance from wood to plastic. At various times in U.S. history coin shortages plagued the nation. As America expanded westward and subsidiary coinage was in short supply from 1832 to 1844, many merchants issued tokens. Typically they would bear the name of the merchant or company and its location, along with a value. Those issued from 1832 to 1844 are called Hard Times tokens. Again during the war years from

American merchants and businesses have issued millions of tokens over the years—some purely for advertising, some "good for" a product or a certain amount of trade.

1860 to 1865, coinage disappeared from circulation (hoarded by citizens nervous about the stability of paper money) and private businesses improvised by issuing what are classified as Civil War tokens. Some of these used design elements of U.S. coins, but state an amount good in trade.

Today tokens continue to be issued for fares for various forms of transportation, for use in commissaries, and for amusement parks. Tokens historically have also been widely used in the gaming industry and are known as gaming chips. Through the years tokens have been issued at various levels of government as evidence of payment for various goods and services, such as tax receipts. Many of these types of tokens are avidly collected. Values can be found at major online auction sites as well as price guides published by collector organizations. A good introduction and overview reference is Katherine Jaeger's *Guide Book of United States Tokens and Medals*.

FOREIGN COINS

It is not unusual to find coins issued by other countries in collections or among items in an estate of a U.S. citizen. Military personnel and those who travel to foreign countries typically save as souvenirs examples of each denomination from countries they visit. Sometimes people become interested in another country's coinage because they or their ancestors immigrated to the United States and obtaining and collecting coins is a way of linking to their heritage.

Generally foreign coins gathered from circulation, especially those that do not contain any silver or gold, carry little to no collector value.

From the late 1950s through the late 1980s collecting world crowns was popular in the United States. The term *crown* generally refers to a coin ranging in size from 36 to 42 mm in diameter. (Crowns and half crowns were also coin denominations in Great Britain.) The larger coins composed of 90 percent silver were the most avidly collected. Also, larger-sized gold coins were popularly collected. Many enthusiasts boasted collections comprising coins from at least 200 countries. While some Americans still collect crown coins of the world, this specialty's popularity has waned since the late 1980s.

Many collectors interested in coins from other countries purchase Uncirculated and Proof sets directly from foreign mints, which aggressively market their commemorative coins and other collectibles in the United States. Thus, it is entirely possible to encounter significant numbers of foreign coins in collections or accumulations of coins of persons living in the United States.

In general, foreign countries follow the same conventions as the United States with regard to coinage. The name of the issuing country is stated on the coin, along with the denomination and year of issue.

There are a number of Internet sites that are useful in identifying and valuing world coins. Two are free and include images and current values for world coins produced after 1600. They are Don's World Coin Gallery (www.worldcoingallery.com) and the NGC World Coin Price Guide (www.ngccoin.com/poplookup/World-Coin-Price-Guide.aspx).

Krause Publications publishes value guides for world coins divided by centuries. The books are sold in bookstores and hobby shops throughout the nation and are often available in public libraries. Various value guides and books about world coins are also available from Whitman Publishing.

Many U.S. coin collections also include at least a few coins from other countries. These might be stored loose in bags or envelopes; stapled into coin holders, with their dates and denominations noted; or displayed in their original mint packaging.

CHAPTER 9

CREATING
AN INVENTORY

M ost of the basic terms used in identifying
your coins or paper money will be used in
your inventory listing. Inventories can be
hand-written or created electronically using a computer. Using a computer is advantageous, especially if
you are dealing with a large quantity of coins. However, the method you choose depends on your skills
and the availability of a computer and software.

Practicality is also a consideration. If you have just
a few items, a legal pad and a pen may suffice. However, if you have hundreds or thousands of coins to
identify and inventory, a computer is an excellent tool
to use. Laptops and tablets are especially useful since
they are portable and can be used in a vault or facility
where the coins might be stored. Basic spreadsheet
software such as Microsoft Excel works well. Use of a
computer spreadsheet has two important advantages:
value totals can be quickly calculated; and selective

Developing an inventory document is an essential part of valuing your
collection. It can be simple or complex, depending on the types and volume
of coins, paper money, and other collectibles you have. Take advantage of
the tips and strategies for keeping this chore simple and easy.

printing of portions of the spreadsheet allows you keep some of the information you have gathered confidential, if it is desirable to do so. Coin-inventory software exists and is used by many collectors. However, such programs are expensive and contain many features that you are unlikely to need to create a basic inventory.

The design of the inventory instrument you use can be very simple or of varying degrees of complexity, depending on the quantity and kinds of coins in the collection and the purpose of the inventory. If you have a few dozen coins, with possibly some from another country, a simple inventory is perhaps all that you will need. The fundamentals are the same, whether writing by hand or using a computer.

COINS

At the top of the page or spreadsheet, give the collection a name. Usually the name reflects the person who collected the coins, especially if the coins are from that person's estate. However, the collection can be given a general name, perhaps reflective of an interest or geographic location. It is important to note who conducted the inventory and when. The year (or month and year) the inventory was completed are generally sufficient.

A basic coin inventory should include columns for Country, Denomination, Date, Design Type, and Mintmark. Additional columns are useful, such as Quantity and Value, and can be added later. Use column headings across the top of the page, such as illustrated here.

A.B. Smith Collection, inventory completed January 2014 by Joe Smith						
Country	Denomination	Date	Design Type	Mintmark	Quantity	Value
USA	Cent	1820	Liberty Head	None	1	
USA	Cent	1866	Indian Head	None	1	
USA	Cent	1942	Lincoln	S	3	
USA	5 Cents	1883	Liberty Head	None	1	
USA	Dime	1941	Winged Liberty	S	1	
Canada	10 Cents	1954	Elizabeth II		2	
USA	Quarter	1954	Washing.	D	1	

If you are creating an inventory for coins from an estate, chances are you will need additional information, so it is best to design your inventory document from the outset to include all needed information. It may be useful to add columns such as Date Acquired, Purchase Price, Grade, and Current Value. If you choose to prepare a handwritten inventory, be sure to list the column headings at the top of each page and number the pages. Some of the information such as the date acquired and the purchase price may be available from bills of sale, invoices, or information noted on the holders containing the coins. More on grading and estimating current value is provided in chapter 10.

A.B. Smith Collection, inventory completed January 2014 by Joe Smith								
Country	Denomination	Date	Design Type	Mintmark	Quantity	Date Acquired	Purchase Price	Current Value
USA	Cent	1820	Liberty Head	None	1	1989	$15	
USA	Cent	1850	Liberty Head	None	1	1989	$14	
USA	Cent	1858	Flying Eagle	None	1	1993	$140	
USA	Cent	1866	Indian Head	None	1	1995	$55	
USA	Cent	1942	Lincoln	S	3	Pocket change	Face value	
USA	5 Cents	1883	Liberty Head	None	1	1990	$10	
USA	5 Cents	1911	Liberty Head	None	1	1990	$30	
USA	Dime	1941	Winged Lib.	S	1	Pocket change	Face value	
Can'da	10 cts	1954	Eliz. II		2	Trade		
USA	25 cts	1954	Wash.	D	1	Pocket change	Face value	

If the person who collected or saved the coins traveled extensively or had an interest in a country other than the United States, you could encounter coins from other lands. If there is a significant quantity, it may be helpful to create a separate inventory for coins not produced in the United States. You could use the same format as the basic inventory. Without additional reference books, you might not have the ability to identify the design type or mintmark, but it would be helpful to record any information that is on the coin. The country of origin, denomination, and date are on all coins. Also, you may be able to identify the primary coinage metal. Documentation such as bills of sale, invoices, and notes written on the coin's holder may provide additional information. It is advisable to record whatever is available.

Country	Denomination	Date	Metal	Purchase Price	Current Value
Iran (Persia)	5 rial	1934	Silver		
Spain	100 pesetas	1966	Silver		
Philippines	1 peso	1965	.900 silver		
Ecuador	5 sucres	1944	Silver		
Jamaica	5 shillings	1966	Copper-nickel		
Portugal	X reis	1791	Copper		
Straits Settlements	1 dollar	1904	Silver		
Latvia	5 lati	1931	Silver		
Canada	1 dollar	1972	.500 silver		
Isle of Man	25 pence	1972	Copper-nickel		
Mexico	1 peso	1947	.500 silver		
Tonga	1 pa'anga	1967	Copper-nickel		

A.B. Smith Collection, inventory completed January 2014 by Joe Smith

If the collection is exclusively United States coins or paper money, you could include that information in the title of the collection. Adding "U.S. Coins" to the title will convey the country of origin so there would be no need for a separate country column. If there are significant quantities of various denominations, it may be useful to modify the basic inventory design by creating separate inventories by denomination. If the inventory is hand-written, be sure to identify the denomination clearly at the top of each page. Computer spreadsheet programs are particularly useful for recording large quantities of various denominations. For example, Microsoft's Excel structure is set up as a "workbook" and provides the ability to have multiple spreadsheets within a workbook. The illustrated workbook is organized by denomination (note the tabs at bottom for various denominations) with the design types listed within each denomination. The first illustration shows the dime spreadsheet,

with several dates and mintmarks listed for each of three design types—
Barber, Winged Liberty, and Roosevelt. If there is evidence of complete
collections and multiples of dates of a particular denomination and multiple design types, it may be advantageous to list all dates and mintmarks
known for each design type as you set up the inventory sheet, such as
shown in the second illustration.

Coin price guides and coin checklists or ledgers that list U.S. coins chronologically by denomination, design type, and mintmark are the best sources for obtaining information about the years specific coins were produced and which mint facilities struck them. These resources are available online, at selected newsstands, and in many bookstores. Since you have obtained a copy of at least one price guide (recommended in chapter 2 as an essential tool), you have all of the information you will need to develop this type of inventory. Very few individuals attempt to collect all known denominations and design types, so your task will not likely be as daunting or time consuming as you might think.

If most of the coins are in folders and albums, creating a separate inventory by denomination / design type may be desirable if you are using the hand-written method. If you are using spreadsheets within a computer workbook, you can add a section within the design type for folders and albums or develop a separate spreadsheet. Since folders and albums are organized by denomination and design type, with holes or slots for each year and mintmark the coin was produced, a shortcut can be taken with the inventory, especially if the folder or album is complete or nearly so. Instead of listing every coin in the album, you can list the dates/mintmarks that are *not* in the album. It is important to understand that folders and albums are created for long shelf life and often carry advance dating. Most have holes for the basic issues of mint facilities that normally produced coins for circulation. Folders and albums produced early in a design-type cycle might not have a hole for a popular die variety discovered after the folder was printed or the album was manufactured. For example, Lincoln cent, Wheat Reverse, folders and albums printed prior to 1955 have slots for 1955 (cents made at the Philadelphia Mint that carried no mintmark), 1955-D (struck at the Denver Mint), and 1955-S (struck at the San Francisco Mint). However, they do not have a slot for the 1955 Doubled Die cent. Once the variety was discovered and it became apparent there were likely enough available that many people would collect them, folder and album manufacturers included a spot for the 1955 Doubled Die in some of their next offerings. Varieties and errors are constantly being discovered, even among earlier dates, as specialists find them and publish information about them. The most widely collected and popular varieties and errors are included in general price guides, but they might not be included in some folders and albums.

	A	B	C	D
1	A.B. Smith U.S. Coin Collection, inventory completed January 2014 by Joe Smith			
2	CENTS FOLDERS			
3				
4	**Design Type**	**Missing Coins**		
5	Flying Eagle	1856		
6				
7	Indian Head	1877; 1888, 8 Over 7; 1909-S		
8				
9	Lincoln			
10	Wheat Reverse 1909-1940	1909-S V.D.B., 1914-D, 1922 No D, 1931-S		
11	Wheat Reverse 1941-1958	1955 Doubled Die		
12	Memorial Reverse 1959-1982	1960-D Small Date, 1972 Doubled Die		
13	Memorial Reverse 1983-2008	1983 Doubled Die, 1995 Doubled Die		
14				
15				
16				
17				
18				
19				

Numismatic books can be valuable, too. Make an inventory of titles and copyright dates.

PAPER MONEY

An inventory for U.S. paper money is similar to one for U.S. coins, whether you're creating a hand-written inventory or a spreadsheet on a computer. Columns in a basic paper-money inventory should include: Type, Denomination, Series, Signatures, Grade, Quantity, and Value. Other information columns may be needed, depending on the type of note. Many price guides and most collectors use the cataloging system developed by Robert Friedberg and continued by his sons, Arthur L. Friedberg and Ira S. Friedberg. If there are references or notes with an F and a number, chances are it is a Friedberg number. Thus it would be prudent to add a column in the inventory for Friedberg numbers and to use a price guide that includes the Friedberg numbering system.

A.B. Smith U.S. Paper Money Collection, inventory completed January 2014 by Joe Smith						
TYPE/DENOMINATION						
Federal Reserve Note/$100						
Friedberg No.	Series	Signatures	Issuing Bank	Grade	Quantity	Value
F 2171A	1985	Ortega/Baker	Boston			
F 2171B	1985	Ortega/Baker	New York			
F 2171B★	1985	Ortega/Baker	New York			
F 2171C	1985	Ortega/Baker	Philadelphia			
F 2171D	1985	Ortega/Baker	Cleveland			
F 2171D★	1985	Ortega/Baker	Cleveland			
F 2171E	1985	Ortega/Baker	Richmond			

TOKENS AND MEDALS

The basic coin-inventory model can be adapted for tokens and medals.

Tokens are privately issued money substitutes, so they have some of the same attributes as coins. A typical token inventory would include columns such as Issuer, Type, Design, Date, Stated Value, Metal Alloy, and Current Value. There are many kinds of tokens and they are generally collected by type. Examples include transportation, merchant, mining, and tax tokens, to name but a few.

Medals generally are commemorative and are issued to honor individuals, groups of people, anniversaries, or events. Historical medals are usually round, but can be oval, rectangular, or even square. Often medals are struck or cast in various alloys and of various sizes. Private individuals, organizations, businesses, and different levels of government issue medals. For example, the U.S. Congress from time to time authorizes a national gold medal to honor an individual or group of people in recognition of their heroic deeds or contributions to the nation or to mankind. This is known as the Congressional Gold Medal. The recipient usually receives the gold version, which is three inches in diameter. The U.S. Mint is authorized to strike bronze duplicates in two sizes—three inches and one-and-a-half inches in diameter—for sale to the public.

A second type of medal is called the art medal. These are produced by artists and sculptors. In fact, art medals are sometimes referred to as "art you can hold in your hand." Art medals are produced in various sizes and shapes. Topics and themes are endless in that there are no bounds other than what can be conceived in the minds of the artists who create them. Generally art medals are made of alloyed metals, but they sometimes include other substances as well.

A third type of medal is the military award, decoration, or badge (all of which are generically referred to as "medals"). All branches of the U.S. Armed Forces (and the armed forces of other countries as well) award medals in recognition of various accomplishments. Generally they are held by the individual who received the award, or their family members. Sometimes military medals enter the secondary market, and they are avidly collected. (Beware of copies and counterfeits.)

General guidelines for creating an inventory for medals would include columns for Design, Artist/Sculptor, Manufacturer, Date, Size, Metal, and Value. In general most medals carry a date, but some do not. Often there is an inscription noting the name of the recipient and the date awarded.

10

DETERMINING VALUE

A fter sorting, identifying, and listing coins in your inventory, you are ready to begin determining how much they are worth in the current market.

There are several components of value for coins but, contrary to popular perception, *age* is not one of them. Some coins minted more than 2,000 years ago are readily available and can be purchased for less than $50. Such coins are great conversation pieces, fun to collect, and of tremendous educational value, but they are unlikely to greatly increase in value in the foreseeable future. Compare them to a modern coin struck by the U.S. Mint in 1995 that carries a face value of $1, contains one ounce of silver, sold for more than $86,000 in March of 2013, and will likely continue to appreciate in value for years to come. How can this be?

In this example, the coin that is more than 2,000 years old is the "poor widow's mite," of biblical fame. Mite was never a denomination and modern scholars

There are four basic components in determining value: mintage, rarity, demand, and grade. Learn how each component factors into the value of your coins and how to use wholesale and retail price guides to get a good estimate of their current market value.

believe the word came into being during translation of the New Testament into English (authorized by King James I of England and completed in 1611). In Jesus' parable a poor widow donates two tiny coins to the temple treasury, while the rich donate much more. Jesus explains that the small sacrifices of the widow mean more to God than do the extravagant—but proportionately less important—donations of the wealthy. From the context of the story (Mark 12: 41–44), it is clear that Jesus was referring to the smallest-value bronze coins in circulation in Jerusalem. This may have been a half-prutah or prutah of Herod the Great, or a prutah issued by a Roman prefect, such as Pontius Pilate (26–36 AD), who ruled after Herod. The tiny bronze coins were issued in massive numbers. Many widow's mites available in the market today are those of the later Hasmonean kings, such as Alexander Jannaeus (103–76 BCE). These are still being unearthed in Israel by the thousands.

The modern coin is the 1995-W Proof American Silver Eagle, the first of the silver bullion coins to bear the West Point mintmark. It was promoted as a "bonus" by the U.S. Mint and included with four American Gold Eagle Proof bullion coins in a special set honoring the 10th anniversary of the 1985 law authorizing the American Eagle gold and silver bullion-coin programs. The Mint sold the set in 1995 for $999, which collectors at the time considered overpriced. The set contained these American Gold Eagle coins: 1 ounce (denominated as $50), 1/2 ounce ($25), 1/4 ounce ($10), and 1/10 ounce ($5), for a total of 1.85 ounces of gold. The world price of gold at the time was averaging around $380 per ounce. The .999 fine American Silver Eagle coin contained 1 ounce of silver, with the average price of silver at $5.20 an ounce. U.S. coin collectors, whose pocketbooks were already stressed by a deluge of recent commemorative coins (including 18 honoring the 1996 Atlanta Olympic Games) and other offerings that year, complained that the Mint was price gouging by asking $999 for the five coins containing slightly more than $708 worth of precious metals. Consequently, most collectors opted not to purchase the set, and only 30,125 were sold. Since the 1995-W Proof American Silver Eagle was only available in the 10th anniversary Proof set, a modern rarity was instantly created. Amer-

ican Silver Eagle bullion coins had become one of the most widely collected U.S. coins of all time in just a decade, with many collectors
purchasing both the bullion-strike and Proof versions annually. Suddenly hundreds of thousands of collectors were chasing the 30,125
Proof silver coins in the sets, and prices for the sets as well as the individual silver coins (which had been removed from the sets by collectors
and dealers) soared. At the top tier of the market were the highest-
graded of the 1995-W Proof American Silver Eagles.

The widow's mite mentioned in the Bible—a coin so ancient and so
famous that it must be extremely valuable. . . or is it? (Shown enlarged.)

The 1995-W American Silver Eagle, issued in a set of modern bullion coins. Is there any chance this coin could be worth more than a widow's mite? (Shown enlarged.)

The 1995-W American Silver Eagle bullion coin is an excellent example of the component attributes that comprise value: low original mintage (quantity produced), high demand, and grade rarity. (For coins that once circulated, surviving supply is also a prime factor in rarity.)

Low original mintage. In the nine years preceding 1995, Proof American Silver Eagle yearly mintages ranged from a high of 1,446,778 to a low of 372,168. Thus we can deduce that prior to 1995, at least 372,168 complete sets of Proof American Silver Eagles could be formed. But the 1995-W Proof coin was a game changer. Suddenly only 30,125 complete sets could be formed. Thus, the 1995-W coin became the key date of the series.

High demand. Demand for the 1995-W Proof American Silver Eagle soared as soon the low mintage number became public. Collectors intent upon keeping their collections complete considered it a must-have. Suddenly hundreds of thousands of collectors were in pursuit of the 30,125 available coins.

Grade rarity. Grade refers to level of preservation, benchmarked on a scale from 1 to 70, with 1 being so worn that it is difficult to see all of the design elements or even all of the date on the coin, and 70 being absolute perfection in striking and pristine surfaces absent any marks or blemishes. Modern minting technology (especially since the mid-1980s) has improved striking capabilities, and attention to careful handling and packaging within minting facilities has resulted in much higher-quality coins reaching the market. In fact, Proof American Eagle bullion coins get the white-glove treatment within the minting facility that produces them. The top professional third-party grading services report on a regular basis the grades they assign to coins submitted for grading. In general approximately 70 to 80 percent of the bullion coins are awarded a grade of 69, with fewer than 10 to 15 percent receiving the perfect 70. Thus, the differential of *grade rarity*. The current collector market is obsessive regarding grades at the top of the scale or the highest grade known for a particular denomination or design series. This is because many collectors strive for the highest quality (grade) they can afford. In late April 2014, a 1995-W American Silver Eagle bullion coin graded Proof-69 Ultra Cameo by Numismatic Guaranty Corporation was listed in NGC's price guide at $4,450, whereas one graded Proof-70 Ultra Cameo by NGC was listed at $18,000. Professional Coin Grading Service, perceived by many collectors as practicing stricter grading, reported in April 2014 that since 1995 it had awarded the grade of Proof-70 Deep Cameo to only 30 of these coins, whereas 1,887 had been graded PFDC-69. (The number of PF-70 grades awarded for this coin was even smaller than the historic average for the overall series, thus setting up the extreme grade rarity.)

1995-W Proof Silver American Eagles Graded

Grade*	NGC	PCGS	Total
Proof 68	181	624	805
Proof 68+	0	1	1
Proof 69	3,740	1,887	5,627
Proof 70	347	30	377

* NGC uses Ultra Cameo designation; PCGS uses Deep Cameo. *Source:* NGC and PCGS population reports as of April 23, 2014.

In April 2014 the PCGS Price Guide listed the PFDC-69 1995-W American Silver Eagles at $3,950 and PFDC-70 versions at $50,000. These examples point out the difference one point on the grading scale can make, as well as premiums at play, depending on which service grades the coin. With so few of the top grades being available in the marketplace, completion is keen. During a March 31, 2013, auction conducted by GreatCollections, a 1995-W American Silver Eagle graded by PCGS as PFDC-70 sold for $86,654.70.

The difference in market value and potential appreciation between the poor widow's mite and the 1995-W Proof American Silver Eagle provide some insight and perspective with regard to valuing coins. While rarity and availability play a role in value, ultimately demand is the key driver of price or value. The poor widow's mite is old and interesting, yet it is available in sufficient quantities to keep prices (values) low because demand does not exceed supply. Given the fact that these small bronze coins are still being found in hoards at archeological digs, it appears an available supply will continue in the future. The 1995-W Proof American Silver Eagle, on the other hand, has a known, limited quantity (mintage) and additional specimens cannot be legally produced. As long as the series is popularly collected and emphasis remains on grade rarity, potential value increases can be expected.

Comparison of the poor widow's mite and a modern U.S. bullion rarity may seem to be an extreme, but this scenario occurs more often than you might think within U.S. federal coins made from 1792 to today. Many of the coins produced within the first 50 years the U.S. Mint was in operation have small mintages, and rarity ratings indicative of small survival rates. But surprisingly many of these coins can be purchased for comparatively modest prices, especially in lower grades, due to the fact that fewer people collect them, resulting in less demand. Yet, coins produced within the last 50 years that have low mintages and are popularly collected—especially in very high grades—carry surprisingly high values.

Many coins cherished by collectors and actively traded in the U.S. coin market were initially struck for circulation and used in commerce. The number produced can be ascertained by reviewing records kept by the government facilities that produced them. Fortunately, mintages for U.S. coins are easily obtained since retail-price guidebooks such as the Red Book have compiled the information from government documents and list mintages by denomination and mint.

While mintages provide an initial snapshot, they must be treated as only one piece of the puzzle. Compared to those of the 21st century, mintages for certain years of some denominations—especially in the 18th and early 19th centuries—are very small. Of more importance for valuing is how many have *survived*, in what condition they have survived, and whether they are avidly collected today.

Rarity, or survival rate, is difficult to determine because there is always the possibility of a hoard being found. No better example can be cited than the 1903-O Morgan dollar. Mintage records show that 4,450,000 were struck for circulation. For decades it was considered the rarest and most desirable of all Morgan dollars. Researchers believed that most of the 1903-O Morgan dollars had been melted under provisions of the 1918 Pittman Act. As the new year dawned in 1962, the collector community believed that fewer than a dozen specimens existed in Mint State grades. Even in circulated grades, the date and mintmark was considered difficult to find. Then came the "great silver rush" beginning in the fall of 1962 and extending through March of 1964, as the U.S. Treasury Department sold off its hoard of silver dollars that had been stored deep within its vaults for more than 50 years. Suddenly dozens of bags, each containing 1,000 1903-O Morgan dollars, were entering the marketplace—all in Mint State. No one knows for sure the exact total, but numismatic researchers estimate from 60,000 up to as many as one million 1903-O Morgan dollars entered the marketplace by early 1963. Almost overnight, the coin's value plummeted. Prior to the Treasury Department's hoard release, the 1903-O Morgan dollar in Mint State retailed for $1,500. Once the coin market began to fathom the numbers of 1903-O Morgan dollars available, prices tumbled to a range of $13 to $15. In 2014, it was possible to purchase a 1903-O Morgan dollar in the $425 to $500 range, depending on the grade, whereas had it remained the key to the series, you would have to add at least two, possibly three, zeros to the price.

For decades collectors thought the 1903-O Morgan dollar was a super-rarity. Then, in November 1962, the Treasury opened a Philadelphia Mint storage vault that had been sealed since 1929. Inside: hundreds of thousands of 1903-O silver dollars, as bright and shiny as the day they were minted. (Shown enlarged.)

With respect to collecting, there was a silver lining to the government's sell-off of its silver dollar hoard (most of which were Morgan dollars, 1878–1921). Suddenly hundreds of thousands of people began collecting Morgan dollars. The series was lifted from relative obscurity to become the most popular and most widely collected design series for a period of more than 30 years.

Another more recent illustration of survival rate is the 1857-S Liberty Head gold double eagle. By 1857 the California Gold Rush was in full swing and the U.S. Mint's newly opened production facility in San Francisco near the gold fields was churning out record numbers of gold coins. Records show the San Francisco Mint struck 970,500 $20 gold coins in 1857, more than double the total combined output of double eagles that year at the New Orleans and Philadelphia mints. However, for more than a hundred years, the 1857-S Liberty Head $20 gold coin in grades higher than Extremely Fine–45 were virtually unknown. There are three basic reasons why. First, from the time of minting in the 1850s through the late 1920s, $20 gold coins circulated in commerce and from bank to bank, thus being subject to wear. Second, in 1933, when President Franklin D. Roosevelt took the United States off the gold standard and recalled gold coins, most $20 gold pieces were turned in by the public and melted into bars (still held at Fort Knox in government vaults). Third, as historians were aware, a shipment of newly struck 1857-S double eagles was among the SS *Central America*'s cargo when it sank September 12, 1857, during a hurricane off the North Carolina coast.

The gold coins of the *Central America* were considered lost until they were identified on the ocean floor (along with other gold coins, ingots, and gold dust) on September 11, 1989, by the Columbus-America Discovery Group. Salvage of the treasure was accomplished using newly engineered technology and special techniques to preserve the gold coins. Due to lawsuits dealing with ownership claims, it took more than a decade to bring to market the 1857-S $20 gold coins salvaged from the *Central America*. Surfaces of more than 5,200 of the coins recovered were virtually in the same state of preservation as when they had left the coining press, grading Mint State–60 through 67. Within the collector market, the history of the coins created a desire to own them, and the hoard was gradually and skillfully disbursed into the marketplace. What had been among the keys to the series was now available in significant quantities. However, prices for the 1857-S $20 gold coins did not take a nose-dive; they have continued to appreciate, due to clever marketing and publicity creating greater demand than the available supply.

Another factor affecting survival rates of gold and silver coins has been run-ups in the prices of precious metals, resulting in melting of coins. As the spot price of silver approached $50 per ounce on January 18, 1980, many speculators and collectors who had "saved back" or plucked circulated 90 percent silver (pre-1965) dimes, quarters, half dollars, and dollar coins from circulation in the early 1960s decided it was time to cash in what was referred to as "junk silver." With silver at $50 an ounce, a 90 percent silver dime (containing 0.07 ounce of silver) was worth $3.50; silver quarters, $9; half dollars, $18; and dollars, $38.50. In the later months of 1979 and early months of 1980, massive quantities of U.S. silver coins were melted. Although some individuals sampled and recorded coins being sent to the melting pots, no comprehensive or official records of quantities by denomination, date, and mintmark were kept. Thus, it is impossible to know exactly how many of each design series was "lost" in what was called "the great silver melt."

Another wave of melting began in early 2008. But this time, the focus was on gold. As the year 2000 began gold had opened at $282 an ounce

Among the golden treasures recovered from the wreck of the SS *Central America* were thousands of 1857-S double eagle coins, remarkably preserved by their submersion in the ocean's depths. Before that discovery the 1857-S was considered rare in Mint State.

on world markets. It would take six years (April 2006) for it to break the $600 per ounce barrier. The meandering between $300 and $600 during that period had a mesmerizing effect on the coin market. But by November of 2007 recollections of the frenzied late 1979–early 1980 period began to stir as gold approached its all-time-record high of $850 an ounce, closing November 7 at $833.50 per ounce on the New York Mercantile Exchange. The coin market and gold traders were astounded when gold sailed past the world record and closed at $856.70 on January 2, the first trading day of 2008. Seven days later the coin market's largest buy-sell-trade show of the year opened in Orlando, Florida, with gold at $877 per ounce, and it was evident a new gold rush was under way. Gold in its various forms—coins, bullion bars, jewelry—flowed into the convention center, as the price of gold continued to escalate. The Friday, January 11, close of $891 per ounce prevailed during the weekend. Lower-grade, common-date gold coins of all denominations were sold for melt as well as newly minted U.S. commemorative gold coins and the newly launched 2007 $10 First Spouse coins containing a half ounce of .9999 fine gold. Collectors and dealers who had purchased large quantities of the first three issues (Martha Washington, Abigail Adams, and Thomas Jefferson's Liberty) decided to take their profits. They had purchased Proof coins at

"Junk silver"—common-date .900 fine silver coins—were melted in huge quantities in 1979 and 1980, as the price of silver rose to $50 per ounce.

$429.95 and Uncirculated versions at $410.95 directly from the Mint and were not willing to gamble on what was shaping up to be a softer collector market due to lack of demand. Although mintage records indicate the first three First Spouse coins have the highest mintages (close to the 40,000 limit) their survival rates are quite likely very different.

The Great Recession (2008 to 2010) in the United States and a stubbornly high unemployment rate, combined with continued escalating prices for gold and silver, again made selling gold and silver coins an attractive option for some, especially those who had unexpectedly found themselves unemployed or "underwater" with a home mortgage. The net result is that many silver and gold coins were sent to the melting pot. Again, no one knows for sure how many coins have been melted since precious metals began their meteoric rise in 2008 because no comprehensive records have been kept. When gold eclipses its all-time high of $1,895 (established September 6, 2011) and silver again broaches the $50 per ounce threshold, more gold and silver coins will likely be melted and premiums on the remaining collector coins will gradually increase, if demand continues.

ZEROING IN ON VALUE

While it may seem that the odds are stacked against sellers who are not knowledgeable collectors or professional coin dealers, take heart. You can quickly improve the odds to a level playing field. Anyone who will commit some time to learn the basics (which you are doing by reading this book), and who uses some basic tools, should be able to gain an understanding as to how the coin market functions and be able estimate the wholesale, retail, and bullion values of any U.S. coin. Identifying these values will position you to sell your coins with confidence that you are getting a fair price.

You have already identified your coins by denomination, design type, date, and mintmark. In order to establish value, or worth, you will need to determine the coin's level of preservation, or *grade*.

Grade is a major factor in determining value. Essentially grade is a tool for communicating value. As mentioned earlier, U.S. coins are graded on a scale of 1 to 70, sometimes called the Sheldon numerical system. Dr. William H. Sheldon developed and published his system in 1949 to relate the *state of preservation* of copper large cents to their *market value*. Use of the scale spread from valuing copper coins to the full range of U.S. coins. In the mid 1970s, the largest collector organization in the United States, the American Numismatic Association, brought together the most skilled graders and market leaders to define and codify the system as it was being expanded to apply to all U.S. coins. The effort resulted in the publication in 1977 of *The Official ANA Grading Standards for United States Coins*. ANA grading standards have continued to evolve as the coin market has expanded and moved toward greater precision. They are widely used and are the basis of the standards employed by the major independent third-party commercial grading services.

Circulated Grades

Numbers 1 through 59 (with 1 being the lowest and 59 the highest grade) are reserved for coins that have circulated—those that have received wear or loss of design details as a result of having been passed from hand to hand or having passed through vending machines. Within the circulated range, the adjectival grades (from lowest to highest) are Poor, Fair, About Good, Good, Very Good, Fine, Very Fine, Extremely Fine, and About Uncirculated. Numbers help to further define the adjectival grades.

Adjectival Grade	Numeric Grade Range
Poor	1
Fair	2
About Good	3
Good	4 to 7
Very Good	8 to 11
Fine	12 to 19
Very Fine	20 to 39
Extremely Fine	40 to 49
About Uncirculated	50 to 59

In practical use, not all of the numbers from 1 through 59 are defined or commonly used. For example, the Good range is from 4 through 7, but the most frequently used numbers in the Good range are 4 and 6. The next higher range, Very Good, begins with 8.

Following are the most frequently used circulated grades, with adjective descriptor, the number, and a general description.

Poor–1 (abbreviated as P-1): Design type is identifiable. Only portions of legends or inscriptions on both obverse and reverse are legible. Date may not be readable.

Fair–2 (abbreviated as FR-2): Design type is identifiable, although both sides are worn smooth. Date is readable.

About Good–3 (abbreviated as AG-3): Design elements are in outline. Parts of date and legends on both sides are worn smooth.

Good–4 (abbreviated as G-4): Design elements and legends are visible, but exhibit heavy wear.

Good–6 (abbreviated as G-6): Design elements and legends are visible, with some design details beginning to emerge.

Very Good–8 (abbreviated as VG-8): Design elements on both sides are clear but appear flat and lack details.

Very Good–10 (abbreviated as VG-10): Design elements are worn, but are clearer and bolder.

Fine–12 (abbreviated as F-12): Heavy wear is evident, but all design elements on both sides are clear and bold.

Fine–15 (abbreviated as F-15): Moderate wear is evident, but the entirety of major design elements on both the obverse and reverse must be clear and bold.

Very Fine–20 (abbreviated as VF-20): All major design elements are sharp, although moderate even wear is present.

Very Fine–30 (abbreviated as VF-30): All major design elements are sharp, with light and even wear evident.

Extremely Fine–40 (abbreviated as EF-40): Light wear is detectable on the high points of the major design elements on both sides.

Extremely Fine–45 (abbreviated as EF-45): Very light wear is detectable on the high points of the major design elements.

About Uncirculated–50 (abbreviated as AU-50): Traces of wear can be seen on the high points of the major design elements.

About Uncirculated–55 (abbreviated as AU-55): Slight traces of wear are detectable on the high points of the major design elements.

About Uncirculated–58 (abbreviated as AU-58): Very slight traces of wear are detectable on the high points of the major design elements.

A close reading of these general descriptions points to a parsing of words to distinguish between the grades. For example, what is the measurable difference between "slight" and "very slight" traces of wear? Often within the circulated grades there are benchmarks specific to the design type that relate to how much of the original design remains, and the description associated with a specific grade level will point to specific design devices as a point of reference. For example, many U.S. coin designs feature a female personification of Liberty and depict her wearing a headband or a tiara with the word LIBERTY inscribed on it. One grade may be pegged at being able to read three letters of LIBERTY. The next higher grade level may cite five letters as the critical benchmark. The next higher level may require that the entire word be readable. Then, the next higher grade may require that the word be not only readable but bold. If you are attempting to arrive at a precise circulated grade, it is best to use a grading guide that provides large, color images of each grade level and also provides written descriptions. By comparing your coin visually to the image and checking the areas identified as benchmark criteria in the written text, you should be able to hone in quickly on the grade of your circulated coin.

AU-55

EF-40

VF-20

F-12

VG-8

G-4

AG-3

A coin's design and legends are crisp and detailed in Mint State. Circulation wears the coin down to About Uncirculated, Extremely Fine, Very Fine, and lower grades, with fewer and fewer details visible as it passes from hand to hand.

Tip: Before attempting to grade a coin of a particular design series, study the design by looking closely at the highest grade available of the coin. (Most grading guides provide at least a Mint State–65 example.) Familiarizing yourself with what the full design looks like will help you understand which details on a circulated coin are missing due to wear. Comparing the design details from grade to grade will help you understand and identify the degree of wear.

Uncirculated Grades

The highest numbers on the 1–70 grading scale are the 11 within the Uncirculated range, 60 to 70.

Adjectival Grade	Numeric Grade Range
Poor	1
Fair	2
About Good	3
Good	4 to 7
Very Good	8 to 11
Fine	12 to 19
Very Fine	20 to 39
Extremely Fine	40 to 49
About Uncirculated	50 to 59
Uncirculated	60 to 70

The Uncirculated range is also referred to as Mint State and is abbreviated used with a hyphen preceding the numbers: MS-60, MS-61, MS-62, MS-63, MS-64, MS-65, MS-67, MS-68, MS-69, and MS-70. The Mint State grades are used to describe coins that have never circulated. It is accurate to refer to them as Uncirculated grades, but in grading parlance, they are known as Mint State—coins in the same state as they were in after being struck by the press at the mint, the government facility in which they were manufactured.

A coin that has never circulated cannot exhibit evidence of wear. However, a Mint State coin can have imperfections (e.g., small dings or scratches from contact with other coins in the course of manufacturing, transportation, and storage); also it might be weakly struck and therefore lack details.

Grading Mint State coins requires an understanding of and knowledge about what the perfect coin would be in each design and denomination. But more importantly, it requires being able to discern the 11 increments that separate perfection (70) from the lowest grade of Mint State (60).

There are four components of Mint State grades: surface preservation, strike, luster, and eye appeal.

Surface preservation refers to the condition of the surfaces of both the obverse and reverse of the coin, although generally the obverse side is the most critical in grade determination. Close inspection of most Uncirculated coins, especially on the lower end of the Mint State scale, reveals contact marks from where the coin has collided with other coins or objects as it was falling from the press or later being jostled in bags or large containers. Imperfections could also be present that were created on the coin's surface during various stages of its manufacture. Tiny scratches, referred to as "hairlines," created by abrasive substances or material used in cleaning, may also be present. To accurately grade, you must judge the visual impact of these imperfections and weigh the degree of severity and determine whether the locations of the imperfections seriously detract from the coin's overall appearance. A good rule of thumb is that the smaller the diameter of the coin, the more detrimental are scratches and nicks on the surface of the coin. Larger-diameter coins have a greater probability of receiving scratches, nicks, and marks. Unless such marks are in the prime focal areas of the designs, they do not affect the grade as much as if on a smaller-diameter coin.

If *wear* can be detected on the surface of a coin, it is automatically classified as *circulated*. The easiest way to determine wear is to identify the design high points (as noted in grading guides) and inspect them for evidence of disruption in the surface. Hold your coin by its edges and tilt it from side to side and then slightly on the up-and-down axis. Silver coins with the slightest degree of wear will appear gray at the high points of the design. On copper and gold coins, the surface will appear darker. A change in color and texture of the surface is an indication of loss of luster, which is the first sign of wear. In grading terms, it is referred to as "signs of abrasion on the high points," and it relegates coins that are mark-free and eye appealing enough to warrant, for example, an MS-63 grade back to AU-58.

A Mint State coin may have dings or scratches from coming into contact with other coins during minting, bagging, or storage. Such marks don't reduce a coin to a *circulated* grade, but they do affect whether where it's graded on the MS-60 to MS-70 scale. This Morgan dollar was graded MS-63.

The differences between a Mint State coin and one that has been circulated are obvious.

Luster on a coin's surface is created from the microscopic flow lines as metal moves to fill the die in the striking process. The brilliance of the luster is created by the way the metal reflects light. On an Uncirculated coin, the full luster will roll over the high points. On an About Uncirculated coin the broken luster can be seen without magnification. Even an inexperienced eye will be able to detect slight wear. One point should be kept in mind: many Mint State coins may have slight friction on the high points or in the fields due to coins rubbing against each other in rolls or bags as they were packaged for distribution at the U.S. Mint. If the luster is intact, the coin is probably Mint State.

Strike refers to the sharpness and completeness of detail imparted by the dies the instant in which a blank metal disk becomes a coin. A fully struck coin shows all of the elements of the design to the smallest detail. All of the United States' minting facilities, at various times, have had striking problems. Thus, it is important to identify the striking characteristics of each minting facility for each series. Researchers in recent years have published books on nearly every denomination and design series, detailing the characteristics of each date and mintmark. Such research is especially helpful in identifying weak strikes. (For example, many Buffalo nickels made at the San Francisco Mint in the 1920s were weakly struck, so even Mint State examples will have soft or missing details.)

Weakness in strike does not automatically lower a coin's grade. However, those who have not studied a series in-depth may confuse weak strikes with slight wear. If the luster is intact, you are probably looking at a weak strike rather than a coin that is worn from circulation.

Eye appeal is the aesthetic appeal of the coin. It is the most subjective of the four factors. Overall attractiveness forces one to take all of the coin's qualities into consideration and rank and balance them. In general, surface preservation is considered the most important factor and is rated as at least two times more important than the other three factors—strike, luster, and eye appeal—which are weighted equally.

The Mint State grades, with 1-point differentials, are far more nuanced than the circulated grades. The best way to grade your Mint State coins is to compare them to images and check the written criteria that define each

Mint State grade. For most people, grading Mint State coins requires the use of a magnifying glass because the one-point difference in grade hinges on tiny details that are difficult to spot without magnification.

Proof Levels

Proof is not a grade. Rather, Proof in reference to coins connotes a method of manufacture. Proof coins are made especially for the collector market and receive the highest-quality strike possible. A Proof coin starts with a specially prepared blank and is struck on a special press with specially prepared dies. Proof coins are not intended to circulate, hence the same 11 numbers and benchmarks of the grading scale that are used for Uncirculated coins are applied in grading

This 1918-D Walking Liberty half dollar might at first glance appear to be circulated. However, what appears to be *circulation wear* is actually a weak strike—a condition seen on many early-date Denver Mint half dollars of this series. The coin was graded MS-63.

Proof coins: Proof-60, Proof-61, Proof-62, Proof-63, Proof-64, Proof-65, Proof-66, Proof-67, Proof-68, Proof-69, and Proof-70. A Proof coin that shows evidence of damage or circulation wear is referred to as an *impaired Proof* and is usually benchmarked with numbers below 60 on the scale.

Using Grading Guides

If your stash of old coins consists primarily of "Wheaties" (Lincoln cents produced from 1909 through 1958) or later-date Lincoln cents (1959 or later), it's probably not worth your time and money to delve deeply into grading. However, if you have a significant number of older copper coins, pre-1965 silver, or any gold coins among those you want to sell, it will definitely pay to invest in a good coin-grading guide because the grade of a coin is a major factor in its value.

It's probably not worth your time to individually grade every coin in a random accumulation of common-date Wheat cents.

Without a basic understanding of grading and having the ability to accurately estimate the coin's grade within one grade level, you will be at a disadvantage when selling.

If you have older copper, silver, or gold coins, you basically have two options:

1. Find (and pay) an independent appraiser who is a skilled grader. (More on this in chapter 11.)
2. Purchase a good grading guide and invest some time in learning how to use it.

Regardless of which grading guide you choose, use it to evaluate and determine (or estimate) a grade for each of your coins. List your grade estimates in your inventory and then value your coins by referring to the grade columns in the price guide.

USING PRICE GUIDES

Now that you have a basic understanding of grading and have listed an estimated grade in your inventory for each coin, you are ready to begin valuing them. It is important to understand the basic structure of price guides (whether retail or wholesale) and all of the information elements contained in the charts that list coin prices.

Two basic types of price guides are available in the coin market: wholesale and retail. Price guides list a specific value for each coin in a range of grades. However, it is important to understand that the listed price is a "ballpark" number. Look at the values on either side of the grade you are targeting for your coin and you will see a range. Much depends on whether a potential buyer perceives the grade assigned to your coin to be "solid for the grade," somewhat lower, or somewhat higher.

Wholesale price guides are designed for and principally used by dealers who buy and sell coins. Since no dealer is likely to be an expert in all design types and denominations, but must keep current on the market for all coins in order to price coins daily for buyers and sellers with whom he does business, most rely on wholesale price guides developed from information gathered from national dealer trading networks and prices reported from public auctions and private transactions. The most widely used wholesale guides for actively traded U.S. coins are those published weekly by the *Coin Dealer Newsletter*. The CDN price guide for "raw" coins—those that have not been graded and encapsulated by third-party grading services—is commonly known as the Greysheet. CDN also publishes a separate weekly guide, known as the Bluesheet, for "certified" coins (those that have been graded and encapsulated by independent third-party grading services). (Electronic versions of these publications are available, also.) Most coin dealers subscribe to these weekly wholesale pricing publications because they list "bid" and "ask" values for every major type of U.S. coin. *Bid* is the price that dealers are paying to other dealers. *Ask* is the price dealers expect to receive when selling to other dealers. It is important to remember that these prices are within the wholesale market, where transactions are usually conducted in bulk lots between highly knowledgeable traders. Unless you are a high-volume, regular customer or a part-time dealer, is it unreasonable to expect coin dealers to sell coins to you for wholesale prices. The difference between bid and ask in the wholesale market is the dealer's profit margin, which can be very thin for most coins sold wholesale. Most dealers make their living buying coins as close as possible to wholesale prices and selling at retail prices, where profit margins are larger. If you have large numbers of coins to sell, it may be advantageous to purchase a wholesale guide book such as the annual *Handbook of United States Coins*, commonly referred to as the "Blue Book." However, also be aware that in a fast-moving market, a book listing values could lag the market because of being published once a year. The weekly CDN publications are much more timely in listing wholesale prices, but for a casual one-time user are high-priced.

Retail price guides may be better resources for casual collectors and one-time sellers, because more independent pricing sources exist and retail prices are more widely available. Retail prices are those that one can expect to pay when purchasing coins from a dealer or collector. Earlier, we identified the retail price guide as being one of your essential tools.

The most widely available price guide for U.S. coins is *A Guide Book of United States Coins*, commonly referred to as the "Red Book." The Red Book is published annually and carries an advance year date.

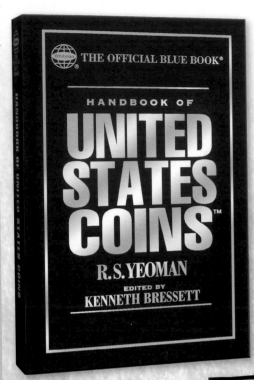

To get a feel for *wholesale* prices—what dealers are paying, on average, to buy U.S. coins if you were to walk into a coin shop or bring your coins to them at a hobby convention—you can refer to the latest edition of the *Handbook of United States Coins.* This popular reference, called the "Blue Book" because of its cover color, has been published since 1942. To reiterate: the Red Book shows retail prices (what you would expect to pay a dealer for a given coin in a given grade), and the Blue Book shows wholesale prices (the "buy price" you can expect a dealer to offer you for a given coin). Be sure to consult the most recent edition.

The Red Book (official title: *A Guide Book of United States Coins*) is available in most bookstores, coin shops, and hobby centers. It can also be purchased online directly from the publisher, Whitman Publishing (www.Whitman.com). The spiral-bound format is handy for inventory purposes. (Hardcover, softcover, large print, and other formats are also available.)

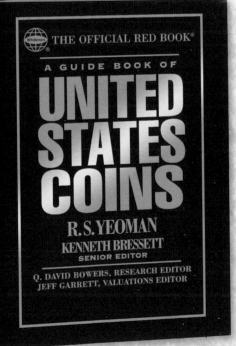

The spread between wholesale and retail prices widens and narrows due to the dynamics of the marketplace and even from dealer to dealer. For example, most dealers have limited supplies of the various dates and mintmarks. When a dealer sells out of a certain date/mintmark, he seeks to replenish his supply. If the coin is popularly collected and other dealers are also seeking the same coin, he may have to increase his bid in the wholesale market. Competition and lack of availability may force wholesale bids higher, with the spread between wholesale and retail becoming narrower. If demand continues as the wholesale bid price escalates, eventually retail prices will increase enough to induce those who own specimens of the coin to sell.

For example, let's look at the 1916 Winged Liberty Head dime in MS-65. The 2015 Blue Book (wholesale) lists an MS-65 1916 Winged Liberty Head dime at $55. The 2015 Red Book (retail) lists the same coin at $120. The difference between wholesale and retail for this coin was $65 when the 2015 editions of these books were published. However, it is important to check current values as you move closer to selling because values and the spread between wholesale and retail may have changed. Obviously, as a seller, you would like to sell the coin for as close to the retail value as possible. (Strategies for selling are discussed in Chapter 14.)

Let's return to the task at hand: completing your inventory by listing an estimated value. Be sure to specify which value you are listing in the value column: wholesale or retail. (If you have access to both wholesale and retail, list both.)

In both wholesale and retail price guides, a range of grades is listed from lowest to highest horizontally across the top of the valuing chart. Due to space considerations, abbreviations are used. For example, in a print publication grades such as AG-3, F-12, VF-20, EF-40, AU-50, MS-60, MS-63, MS-64, MS-65, and MS-66 may be across the top. Electronic price guides may have a greater range of grades, depending on the collecting popularity of the denomination/design series.

In general, all coin price guides present the coins from lowest to highest denominations. For example, in the U.S. federal series, price guides begin with the half cent and continue through the highest denomination produced for circulation, the $20 gold double eagle. (Most price guides also include U.S. commemoratives and modern bullion coins.)

Within each denomination, the coins are listed chronologically by design type. For example, dime is the 10-cent denomination. Each dime design type—Draped Bust (1796–1807), Capped Bust (1809–1837), Liberty Seated (1837–1891), Barber (1892–1916), Winged Liberty (1916–1945), Roosevelt (1946 to date)—comprises a separate section or chart. Within the individual design series, each year of production and producing mint are identified and listed chronologically. Sometimes major and/or popularly collected die varieties (like doubled dies and repunched mintmarks) may also be listed.

In the accompanying illustration, basic information elements within the chart are identified with arrows as reference points.

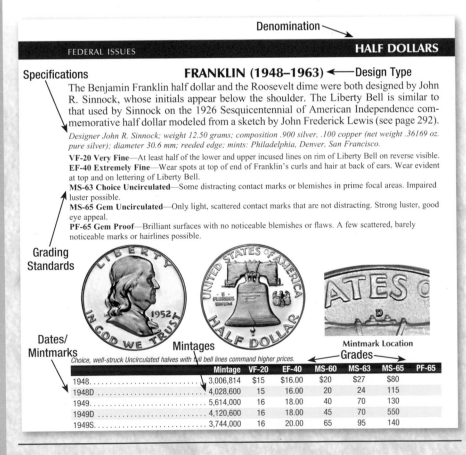

Denomination

FEDERAL ISSUES — HALF DOLLARS

Specifications

FRANKLIN (1948–1963) ← Design Type

The Benjamin Franklin half dollar and the Roosevelt dime were both designed by John R. Sinnock, whose initials appear below the shoulder. The Liberty Bell is similar to that used by Sinnock on the 1926 Sesquicentennial of American Independence commemorative half dollar modeled from a sketch by John Frederick Lewis (see page 292).

Designer John R. Sinnock; weight 12.50 grams; composition .900 silver, .100 copper (net weight .36169 oz. pure silver); diameter 30.6 mm; reeded edge; mints: Philadelphia, Denver, San Francisco.

VF-20 Very Fine—At least half of the lower and upper incused lines on rim of Liberty Bell on reverse visible.
EF-40 Extremely Fine—Wear spots at top of end of Franklin's curls and hair at back of ears. Wear evident at top and on lettering of Liberty Bell.
MS-63 Choice Uncirculated—Some distracting contact marks or blemishes in prime focal areas. Impaired luster possible.
MS-65 Gem Uncirculated—Only light, scattered contact marks that are not distracting. Strong luster, good eye appeal.
PF-65 Gem Proof—Brilliant surfaces with no noticeable blemishes or flaws. A few scattered, barely noticeable marks or hairlines possible.

Grading Standards

Dates/ Mintmarks Mintages Mintmark Location Grades

Choice, well-struck Uncirculated halves with full bell lines command higher prices.

	Mintage	VF-20	EF-40	MS-60	MS-63	MS-65	PF-65
1948	3,006,814	$15	$16.00	$20	$27	$80	
1948D	4,028,600	15	16.00	20	24	115	
1949	5,614,000	16	18.00	40	70	130	
1949D	4,120,600	16	18.00	45	70	550	
1949S	3,744,000	16	20.00	65	95	140	

How to Use a Retail Price Guide

Used properly, a good coin price guide can save you a lot of time and effort as well as provide you with insight regarding the value of your coins.

Since you have prepared an inventory by denomination and design type, listing dates and mintmarks and grades, it is time to begin to use the price guide to discover the value of the coins you have. Look first at the furthest-left column of prices. This would be the column displaying the lowest grade. Scan down the column vertically. Dates and mintmark combinations that have higher values are immediately identifiable.

The illustration (part of page 157 from the 2015 Red Book) shows a portion of Winged Liberty dime chart—1916 through 1921 (Philadelphia Mint). Note that all but two of the prices under the G-4 column range from $3 to $4.50. Two dates, the 1916-D and 1921 (the Philadelphia strike, which does not have a mintmark) almost leap off the page! The 1916-D is the rarest and the key to the Mercury dime series. Even in G-4 is it valued at $1,000.00. Follow the line across to the highest grade listed and you will see how the price escalates at each grade increment, reaching $28,000.00 in MS-65. Chances are that if you have Winged Liberty dimes, they will be "common" dates rather than key or rare dates. However, check out the values for each date-and-mintmark combination you have in your inventory. For example, if you have a 1917-D, it is worth a closer look. While the retail value is $4.50 in G-4, look at the value for an EF-40 specimen—$45!

Uncirculated values shown are for average pieces with minimum blemishes; those with sharp strikes and split horizontal bands on reverse are worth much more.

	Mintage	G-4	VG-8	F-12	VF-20	EF-40	AU-50	MS-60	MS-63	MS-65
1916	22,180,080	$3.50	$5.00	$7.00	$8	$12	$25	$35	$45	$120
1916D	264,000	1,000.00	1,500.00	2,600.00	4,200	6,200	9,200	13,200	17,000	28,000
1916S	10,450,000	4.00	6.00	9.00	12	20	25	42	65	215
1917	55,230,000	3.00	3.25	3.50	6	8	12	30	60	170
1917D	9,402,000	4.50	6.00	11.00	22	45	95	145	350	1,050
1917S	27,330,000	3.00	3.25	4.00	7	12	30	60	180	550
1918	26,680,000	3.00	4.00	6.00	12	25	40	70	125	460
1918D	22,674,800	3.00	4.00	6.00	12	24	50	125	250	600
1918S	19,300,000	3.00	3.25	5.00	10	18	40	120	275	725
1919	35,740,000	3.00	3.25	4.00	6	10	30	45	120	375
1919D	9,939,000	4.00	7.00	12.00	24	35	75	200	450	1,750
1919S	8,850,000	3.50	4.00	8.00	16	35	75	200	450	1,250
1920	59,030,000	3.00	3.25	3.50	5	8	15	35	75	260
1920D	19,171,000	3.00	3.50	4.50	8	20	45	145	350	775
1920S	13,820,000	3.25	4.00	5.00	8	18	45	145	325	1,450
1921	11,230,000	65.00	80.00	130.00	320	600	925	1,200	2,000	3,500

In order to best use your time, it is advisable to first check each series for key or semi-key dates. You can easily spot them by using the lowest grade column and identifying coins by date/mintmark that have much higher values relative to most of the other dates/mintmarks listed within the series. Identify any key dates and place them in proper holders (2-by-2 flips, for example). If you have key dates or semi-key dates, a good strategy would be to grade them first and make sure you separate them and keep them in a safe place. Any key dates that you identify as having a retail value in excess of $100 should be authenticated and graded by a professional coin-grading service. The higher-valued coins (key dates) over the years have been targets for counterfeiters and the unscrupulous who alter coins. Thus, authentication is a must for higher-valued coins.

By checking the dates/mintmarks listed in your inventory and comparing to the price guide, you can determine how much time you need

The 1916-D is the key date to the Winged Liberty dime series; the 1921 also is rare. Collectors value these particular coins even in circulated grades.

or want to spend grading your coins. For example, after looking at images of a particular series in a grading guide, you may be able to determine that most of your coins are common dates and fall within a certain grade range (e.g., from VF-20 to EF-40), and then value them accordingly or on an average.

PROFESSIONAL COIN GRADING SERVICES

Coins that you identify as either rare or having a retail value in excess of $100 are good candidates for submission to a third-party commercial grading service. These services are called *third-party* because they grade coins but are neither the coins' owner nor their potential buyer.

Grading of coins is an art, which has since 1986 become more refined and codified, in large part due to the rise of commercial third-party grading services. However, as scientific it may seem, coin grading is not 100 percent objective. Professional coin grading is performed by human beings and is therefore subjective, open to interpretation. Grades assigned by third-party grading services are opinions rendered by experts—and experts can and sometimes do differ in their opinions.

Sonically sealed, tamper-resistant plastic holders (commonly referred to as "slabs") were introduced on a broad scale in the coin market in 1986. Slabs are designed to keep the grading opinion with the coin; they also function as display devices that protect coins from mishandling. Simultaneous to introduction of the slab in 1986 came the first full use of the 1-to-70 scale, and professional graders willing to back their authentications and grading opinions with a money-back guarantee.

Coin grading is a highly competitive, unregulated business sector of the coin market. Should you decide that your coin is a good candidate for authentication and professional grading, you should also evaluate and determine which grading service best suits your needs.

The following third-party commercial grading services are among the leading services by volume of coins graded yearly and by cumulative value of coins graded. Contact the individual grading service directly for information about its submission process and fees. Be sure to also check out each service's authentication and grading guarantee.

Slabs protect coins and offer a permanent record of their grades.

Professional Coin Grading Service (PCGS), a division of Collectors
    Universe Inc. (NASDAG:CLCT)
Professional Coin Grading Service, PO Box 9458 Newport Beach, CA
    92658.
Telephone: 800-447-8848.
Web site: www.pcgs.com
Email: info@pcgs.com

Numismatic Guaranty Corporation of America (NGC)
Numismatic Guaranty Corporation, PO Box 4776, Sarasota, FL 34230.
Telephone: 1-800-NGC-COIN toll free, or 1-941-360-3990.
Web site: www.ngccoin.com
Email: info@ngccoin.com

ANACS
ANACS, PO Box 6000, Englewood, CO 80155.
Telephone: 1-800-888-1861 toll free, or 303-339-3400.
Web site: www.anacs.com
Email: customerservice@anacs.com

Independent Coin Graders (ICG)
Independent Coin Graders, PO Box 276000, Tampa, FL 33688.
Telephone: 1-877-221-4424 toll free, or 813-963-2401.
Web site: www.icgcoin.com
Email: customersatisfaction@icgcoin.com

SEGS Inc. (SEGS)
SEGS, PO Box 8129, Chattanooga, TN 37411.
Telephone: 1-888-768-7261 toll free.
Web site: www.segsgrading.com
Email: segscoins@gmail.com

BULLION VALUE

A third value column that may be helpful to add to your inventory is for bullion value. Earlier we discussed wholesale and retail values for coins that have "collector value" due to their rarity, grade (state of preservation), or collector activity. However, many coins exist that have little collector value but are worth far more than their face value, which is the amount stated on the coin. In coin-market nomenclature, such coins are often referred to as "common date" or even "junk" coins. Some price guides do not attempt to price them and simply use the term BV (for bullion value).

Bullion value is sometimes referred to as melt value or intrinsic value. The three terms are synonymous and refer to the value of the metal or metals contained within the planchet on which the coin was struck. In practical terms, when referring to U.S. coins, melt value is most applicable to silver and gold coins.

As the prices of industrial metals such as copper, nickel, and zinc began to rise in 2005 and 2006, many people who had been hoarding large quantities of 95 percent copper Lincoln cents (those produced prior to 1982) thought they might be able to sell their holdings for their copper value. However, the escalating prices also began to affect current production of one-cent and five-cent coins, because the costs to produce the two denominations rose to exceed their face values. Except for a brief period during World War II, the five-cent coin has been comprised of 75 percent copper and 25 percent nickel. Due to the escalating price of copper in the early 1980s the composition of the one-cent denomination was switched from 95 percent copper to 97 percent zinc with a copper coating to retain the copper color. Since many Lincoln cents dated prior to 1982 continued to circulate in the first decade of the 21st century, mass melting of the denomination could have greatly impacted the U.S. Mint's ability to continue to produce enough cents to meet the needs of commerce. Thus, the secretary of the Treasury issued interim regulations (which have the effect and force of law) that prohibit the exportation, melting, or treatment of United States one-cent coins and five-cent coins. The interim regulation became effective upon publication in the Federal Register on December 20, 2006. After a period of public comment, the regulation became final with publication on April 16, 2007. Violation of the regulation is punishable by a fine of up to $10,000, imprisonment of up to five years, and forfeiture of the subject coins or metal. (Authority for implementing such regulations is in Title 31 of the United States Code, Section 5111(d).)

There are no such prohibitions against melting U.S. coins made of silver and gold, primarily because most have long ceased to circulate in

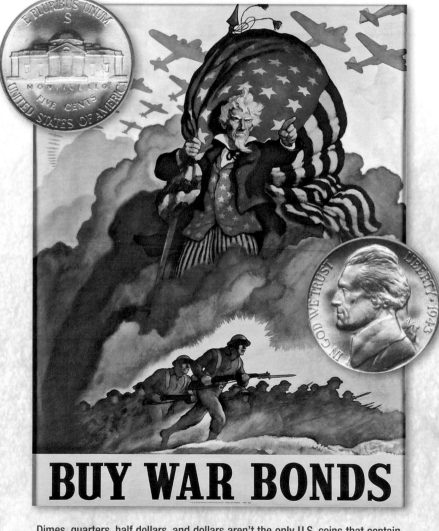

BUY WAR BONDS

Dimes, quarters, half dollars, and dollars aren't the only U.S. coins that contain silver. During World War II, in order to conserve copper for the war effort, the Mint made its five-cent coins out of manganese and silver. The new coins featured a large-sized mintmark above Monticello. (Coin shown enlarged.)

commerce and their melting would not impact the U.S. Mint's production of circulating coins for commerce.

U.S. dimes, quarters, and half dollars produced for circulation from 1837 to 1964 are 90 percent silver. Also made of 90 percent silver are U.S. dollars produced from 1837 to 1935 and U.S. commemorative dollars made in 1900 and from 1983 to date. U.S. denominations from the half dime through the dollar from 1792 to 1835 are made of 89.24 percent silver. Kennedy half dollars dated 1965 to 1969 are made of 40 percent silver. Some Eisenhower dollars included in Uncirculated and Proof sets were made of 40 percent silver from 1971 to 1974 and again in a special Bicentennial set in 1976. Jefferson wartime five-cent coins produced from 1942 to 1945 contain 35 percent silver.

Since 1992 the U.S. Mint has also produced Silver Proof sets containing 90 percent silver dimes, quarters, and half dollars, as well as silver versions of the 50 State quarters, the D.C. and Territorial quarters, and quarters in the America the Beautiful series.

The Mint began annual production of the .999 fine American Silver Eagle bullion coins in 1986. Many of the bullion-strike versions (especially those produced in recent years that have exceedingly high mintages) sell for only a small premium above the spot price of silver. (Spot price is the current, continuously fluctuating market price of a precious metal, determined by the latest trading on the futures market and over-the-counter markets.) However, Proof versions (struck in relatively smaller quantities for collector demand) of the American Silver Eagle bullion coins trade significantly above bullion value.

Most U.S. gold coins produced prior to 1934 contain 90 percent gold and that standard has continued to be used for commemorative gold coins. However, modern gold bullion coins are being produced on different standards. American Gold Eagle bullion coins are 91.67 percent gold. American Buffalo gold bullion and the First Spouse gold coins are 24-karat gold (.9999 fine). See chapter 5 for more information.

Since 1997 the U.S. Mint also has produced and sold American Platinum Eagle bullion coins, which are .9995 fine.

It is possible to individually calculate the bullion value of any U.S. coin as long as you know the weight of the coin in troy ounces, the percentage of precious metal it contains, and the spot price of the precious metal:

weight × percentage of precious metal × price per ounce = bullion value

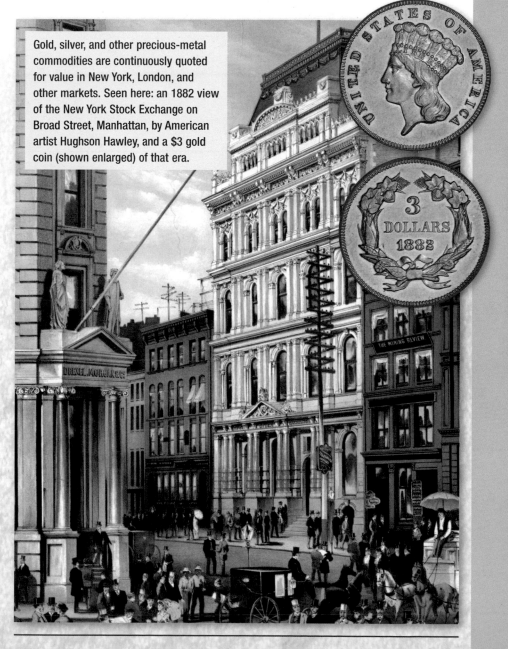

Gold, silver, and other precious-metal commodities are continuously quoted for value in New York, London, and other markets. Seen here: an 1882 view of the New York Stock Exchange on Broad Street, Manhattan, by American artist Hughson Hawley, and a $3 gold coin (shown enlarged) of that era.

The weight and percentage of precious metal(s) are listed in the coin identification section (chapter 5). The spot price of precious metals is available from a multitude of sources on the Internet, updated every 20 minutes when the markets are open. Prices are also published daily in financial publications such as the *Wall Street Journal*. If you don't have time to calculate each coin type individually, using a site such as www.coinflation.com can be the answer.

Some coin dealers use the previous day's close of precious metals in calculating their buying prices for "melt" value coins, although others are able to quote "live" as the metals are trading. Although precious metals trade worldwide Monday through Friday, the U.S. markets generally close at 4 p.m. Between-day prices can be volatile. Thus, it would be practical for you to use the market-close price for calculations. If you add a Bullion Value column to your inventory, be sure to make note of the spot price of the predominant metal used in your coin.

In Conclusion, and a Case Study

Taking the time to research the bullion value, wholesale value, and retail value of each of the coins you plan to sell will arm you with great information and prepare you to talk with potential buyers. It is important to understand that the coin market is dynamic and can make significant moves up or down in just a day's time, especially for bullion-sensitive coins. A portion of an inventory for Franklin half dollars is illustrated here to point out several points that you must keep in mind:

- Percentage spreads between the wholesale and retail values for coins can vary from coin to coin.
- Some price guides do not list precious-metals prices at the time the values were being prepared. In that all silver and gold U.S. coins have a minimum value based on the amount of precious metals they contain, it is important to establish a current minimum value for each coin. Using price guides prepared on an annual basis can be tricky, especially in a volatile market. A price guide published monthly, weekly, or daily has a shorter lag time.

Let's examine a portion of the Franklin half dollar inventory illustrated below.

	A	B	C	D	E	F	G	H
1	A.B. Smith U.S. Coin Collection, inventory completed by Joe Smith May 2014							
2	HALF DOLLARS							
3	*Bullion values based on $19.45 per ounce silver; Wholesale, 2015 Blue Book; Retail, 2015 Red Book.							
4	BV=Bullion Value; WV=Wholesale value; RV=Retail value							
5	Franklin							
6	Date	Quantity	Grade	BV*	WV	RV		
7	1948	3	MS-63	$21.09	$42	$81		
8	1948-D	1	EF-40	$7.03	$8	$16		
9	1949	1	EF-40	$7.03	$8	$18		
10	1949-D	1	EF-40	$7.03	$8	$18		
11	1949-S	1	MS-60	$7.03	$25	$65		
12	1950	2	EF-40	$14.06	$16	$60		
13	1950-D	1	MS-60	$7.03	$9	$26		
14	1951	1	EF-40	$7.03	$8	$14		
15	1951-D	1	EF-40	$7.03	$8	$14		
16	1951-S	3	EF-40	$21.09	$18	$42		
17	1952	1	EF-40	$7.03	$8	$14		
18	1952-D	2	MS-63	$14.06	$20	$46		
19	1952-S	1	EF-40	$7.03	$8	$17		
20	1953	1	EF-40	$7.03	$8	$14		
21	1953-D	1	MS-63	$7.03	$10	$23		
22	1953-S	4	MS-60	$28.12	$72	$100		
23	1954	1	MS-60	$7.03	$9	$16		
24	1954-D	1	MS-60	$7.03	$9	$16		
25	1954-S	1	MS-63	$7.03	$11	$26		
26	1955	1	MS-63	$7.03	$12	$35		
27	1956	1	MS-60	$7.03	$9	$16		

The wholesale and retail values provide significant insight as to the spread between market pricing in this series. Note the spread ranges from a high of more than 70 percent to a low of about 26 percent.

If you have a large number of coins to inventory, it is likely you will be working over a period of weeks or even months. In such cases it would be wise to note or highlight dates/mintmarks within in the series that have narrow spreads. If you are handy with spreadsheets you can use a formula to automatically calculate them in an additional column. Then, closer to the time you plan to sell, consult a price guide that has been recently prepared (no more than two to four weeks ago, if possible). Also, when you are ready to sell, check the spot prices of precious metals.

There are at leave five good reasons to seek an independent appraisal for your coins and other numismatic collectibles.

11

INDEPENDENT APPRAISALS

At this point you have developed a complete inventory that identifies the individual coins / numismatic items you have, with estimates of grades and values. This gives you a good "ballpark" indicator of total value. If the items are yours (no one else has an ownership interest or claim upon them), and you want to sell your holdings, you are ready to identify potential buyers.

Before selling your coins, it may pay to be aware of the various tax implications regarding profits (gains) from selling your coins. They are discussed chapter 12.

First, it is important to decide whether you need an independent appraisal and how to obtain it.

There are a number of reasons that it would be prudent or necessary to have an independent appraisal prior to identifying a buyer. Among the reasons:

- The coins / numismatic items are part of an estate or trust that specifies the estate or holdings must be equitably divided.
- You plan to donate your numismatic holdings to a museum or other nonprofit entity.
- You need an independent appraisal for insurance purposes.

- You need an independent appraisal so that you can use the coins / numismatic items as collateral for a loan.
- You want to confirm your work in order to have better bargaining power with potential buyers.

DIVIDING EQUITABLY

In order to "divide equitably," the current market value of the coins and other numismatic collectibles must be determined. If the person who formed the accumulation or collection kept a detailed inventory (including grades) it may be only a matter of checking current retail-price guides to make sure the values listed are consistent with the current market. For example, the deceased collector maintained a comprehensive inventory, but due to health conditions he or she was not able to keep values updated within the past year. However, if the coins and other numismatic collectibles are not identified and ungraded, the services of a person having expert knowledge of the specific collectible(s) and the current market are required. Even if some who stand to inherit or gain from sale of the collectibles have limited or expert numismatic expertise, an independent appraisal will likely be the best route in order to assure fairness and meet requirements specified by the will or trust.

Even if the coins and other numismatic collectibles are not required to be divided equitably, an inventory listing the current market value of all assets of a deceased person is required in settling an estate. Numismatic collections are personal property and assets. Executors or administrators faced with the task of listing the current market value of a numismatic collection, especially when there is no evidence of the collector having kept a current inventory (with valuations), often seek individuals with specialized knowledge to value the collection in order to be able to list the value of the numismatic holdings as a component in the overall value of the estate.

DONATING NUMISMATIC ITEMS

Sometimes those who inherit coins or other numismatic collectibles have no interest in keeping them and don't have the time or inclination to personally sell their holdings. Whether a small accumulation of coins or a large collection, donating them to a museum or other nonprofit entity can be a viable solution. Most museums and nonprofit organizations will sell your donations in order to raise money to support their programs. Of course, if your coins are rare or historically important, museums may wish to add your donation to their collections.

In order to receive a tax deduction for a charitable gift of items such as coins and other numismatic collectibles, the person or entity making the donation is responsible for declaring the fair market value. An independent appraisal is best in such circumstances. Contact the entity to which you would like to donate your holdings for further information and its policy/procedure for donations. Under current federal law, any donation of $5,000 or more requires a formal written appraisal. For donations that have a fair market value of less than $5,000, the donor can determine the fair market value of the donated property.

For tax purposes, generally the amount of a deduction is based on the fair market value of the property (coins and other numismatic collectibles) and not the original cost to the owner. If you are considering a charitable gift for which you intend to take a tax deduction, it may be prudent to involve your tax planner or attorney. A gift of tangible personal property (such as coins and paper money) must relate to the tax-exempt purposes or functions of the receiving organization in order to take maximum advantage of a tax deduction for property that would otherwise be subject to capital gains tax.

For example, if you donate a collection of coins that cost $5,000 but is now worth $20,000 to the American Numismatic Association for the purpose of expanding its museum collections, your deduction would be the current market value since the donation enhances the educational mission of the organization. However, if you donated the collection to the local humane society for its annual capital campaign, you would only be able to deduct your acquisition costs.

Numismatic collectibles can be donated to a museum, research library, or other nonprofit entity for a tax deduction. Both the American Numismatic Association (in Colorado Springs) and the American Numismatic Society (in New York City) maintain museums and numismatic libraries. Both have non-profit status with the IRS.

It may be advisable to request that the qualified organization provide a written acceptance of the collection, stating that the organization qualifies for tax-exempt status and how the organization will use the collection.

Insurance

Absent documentation of ownership and purchase price of your collectibles, insurers generally require an appraisal by a person recognized as an expert in the field or one who has independent appraiser credentials. Since the purpose of insurance is to reimburse you after loss of your property due to theft, fire, flooding, other acts of God, etc., it is important to have an established value before whatever calamity occurs. Most regular homeowner's insurance policies have limits as to the amount to be paid in the event of a loss on collectibles. Thus, it is important to carefully review your policy for adequate coverage. Due to such limitations, many insurance experts recommend supplementary insurance, known as a floater or rider policy, which specifically lists your coins and other numismatic collectibles. Such supplemental policies insure the full value of the specific item(s). There are insurance companies that specialize in coverage of collectibles. Insurance rates vary from state to state. Check with the insurance company or agent for requirements in declaring and documenting the value of coins and other numismatic collectibles. Retail valuations are frequently used because they would be closest to "replacement value" in the event your collection is stolen, destroyed, or damaged and you seek to replace it.

Confirming Your Inventory / Valuing

While it is not necessary, some people like the reassurance of a second opinion, especially that of a knowledgeable person who does not have a vested interest. If you seek an independent appraisal, be sure to advise the person that you intend to sell your coins so that the appraisal will reflect the amount you can realistically expect to receive for your coins.

Finding an Independent Appraiser

There are several key points to keep in mind when you seek the services of an appraiser:

The appraiser should be independent. It is vital that the person performing the appraisal be truly independent and work on your behalf. If an appraiser is setting a value for coins and other numismatic collectibles with the possibility of purchasing them, you are likely to receive low estimates because he or she would have a vested interest and could not claim to be unbiased.

The appraiser should be knowledgeable. Ask for and verify the appraiser's expertise in numismatics—for example, education, experience, and standing with professional or numismatic collector organizations. While the appraiser may have expertise in other collectible fields such as stamps, Old Masters art, or antiques, be sure the appraiser you choose also has relevant certifiable expertise in coins, paper money, and other numismatic collectibles. The Uniform Standards of Professional Appraisal Practice (USPAP) are quality-control standards applicable to personal-property appraisals. In addition to having knowledge of coins, paper money, and other numismatic collectibles, an appraiser should be well informed about the most current USPAP.

Compensation should be spelled out. Independent appraisers are generally paid an hourly rate or sometimes a daily rate. Seek a preliminary estimate based on information you provide (from your inventory) about the number and kinds of items to be appraised. Once you are satisfied with the estimate, seek a written contract that clearly enumerates terms, conditions, and compensation. The final estimate is normally based on the estimated time needed to examine the collection and prepare the written appraisal. Some appraisers may include a provision in their letter of engagement specifying the need for additional compensation should the appraiser be called to testify in a legal proceeding based on the appraisal. Compensation for an appraisal should never be based on the value of the collection.

Numismatic items should remain in the custody of their owner(s). An appraisal should always be performed where the collection is securely stored or housed. (It might be necessary for the appraiser to travel to the location, so compensation for travel may be an item that needs to be agreed upon as one of the terms of the contract.) Under no circumstances should the appraiser ever take control of or possession of any items that are being appraised. You or your representative should be present during the appraisal to observe the process.

Elements of a Competent Appraisal Report

A formal appraisal report should have a cover document explaining the purpose of the appraisal (what type of value is being sought) and how the appraisal is to be used. It should explain the methodology and identify the resources used to determine values, a complete and accurate description of the property (coins, paper money, and other numismatic collectibles) so that it can be clearly identified, and the date and location of the inspection.

Often the effective date of the value may not be the date of inspection. For example, an estate appraisal may list the value on the date of death of the decedent. In all circumstances, coin appraisals should clearly state the bullion prices used when calculating values.

A formal appraisal report should contain a statement by the appraiser that he or she has no financial interest in the property. If the appraiser has an interest, it should be disclosed in the report. The appraiser's qualifications should be listed and his or her signature should be on the report.

If you desire suggestions on the marketability of certain coins, recommendations on which coins should be sent to a professional grading service, or advice as to which auction house would be a good choice to sell your collection, it would be prudent to ask for such information to be contained in a letter separate from the formal appraisal report.

Nationally Accredited Numismatic Appraisers

Surprisingly few individuals have national accreditation as independent numismatic appraisers.

The most prominent and respected appraisal organizations in the United States are: the International Society of Appraisers (www.isa-appraisers.org);

the American Society of Appraisers (www.appraisers.org); and the Appraisers Association of America (www.appraisersassociation.org).

Professional appraisers who are members of a major appraisal organization provide written opinions on value with the value conclusions based on their organization's prescribed methods of evaluation, research, and report writing.

For example, the International Society of Appraisers requires that a candidate pass a week-long Core Course in Appraisal Studies. Upon completing and passing the core course and with three years of related experience, a candidate may become a member. Within five years, a member may become an accredited member by demonstrating advanced knowledge in a specialty field. A Certified Appraiser of Personal Property is the highest level of membership in ISA. ASA and AAA have similar educational programs and requirements. Members of these organizations must also take continuing-education courses to stay current in their field and maintain awareness in changes in appraisal methodology, including participating in USPAP update courses every two years.

Given the quality of images taken with digital cameras and high-quality scanners, some independent appraisers are willing to work using images and information you supply regarding your coins and other numismatic collectibles. Also the use of Skype or FaceTime via computer, tablet, or smart phone can greatly enhance your conversations with an appraiser who is working with you long distance.

There are many coin dealers and advanced collectors or numismatists who have the knowledge and ability to perform appraisals but do not have national accreditation. Such experts often conduct appraisals for local banks, attorneys, and auctioneers. If you choose to seek a local unaccredited numismatic appraiser, check with an officer of your local bank to learn if the bank has used his or her services. Or, check with a coin club in your area for a recommendation. Many coin dealers who perform appraisals often note the fact in the "About Us" section of their web sites.

A fundamental in seeking an appraiser is to clarify that you are seeking an independent appraisal and will not consider selling your coins or paper money to the person who performs the appraisal.

Coins and other numismatic collectibles are generally passed to heirs via a will or through an estate. If the person who formed the collection prepared for the eventuality of his or her demise by leaving a will and a comprehensive inventory of his numismatic holdings (complete with values), the executor will have an easier task when settling the estate. If no inventory exists, one can be created using information provided in chapter 9, values can be determined by using information and sources cited in chapter 10, and an independent appraisal can be obtained by following the guidelines provided in chapter 11.

12

TAXES

The following information regarding the various types of taxes is general in nature and should not be construed to be legal advice regarding taxes. Rather, it is provided to make you more aware of possible taxes related to your estate or coins and collectibles you may inherit or sell. For specific advice regarding your circumstances, it is best to consult your accountant, an attorney specializing in taxes, or an estate-planning professional.

PROBATE

Probate, the procedure for settling the estate of a deceased person, is conducted in and according to the laws of the state in which the deceased maintained legal residence. Probate retitles a deceased person's property and puts it into the designated beneficiary's name. If the deceased person had a will, he or she probably named a person or persons as executor or co-executors. If no one is named executor in the will, the probate court names an administrator (who functions the same as an executor).

The value of the estate is important in determining whether it is subject to various taxes.

Some states require the executor or administrator, within 90 days of being appointed by the court, to prepare what is referred to as the *90-day inventory*. The 90-day inventory lists all property and assets of the deceased and declares a current fair market value of the items. If there are questions regarding values listed on the 90-day inventory they must be resolved by the time the *final inventory* is filed with the court. The final inventory is used in distributing assets of the estate to those named in the will. If no will exists, the estate is distributed to heirs according to state statute (such a situation is called *intestacy*, and the estate is said to be *intestate*).

FEDERAL ESTATE TAX

Property (cash, real estate, stocks, and other assets, including precious metals, coins, and other numismatic holdings) owned by a person at the time of his or her death becomes what is known as the "decedent's estate." When an estate is transferred to heirs, the federal government may collect a federal estate tax. The tax is owed by the estate of the deceased person and is paid by the estate prior to the transfer of the property to recipients or heirs. Those who receive money or property from an estate are not required to pay the estate tax, nor do they pay any income tax on the value of the inherited property.

The estates of most Americans do not require the filing of a federal estate tax return (IRS Form 706—Estate Tax Return) because the combined estate's gross assets and prior taxable gifts do not exceed the exemption established by the American Taxpayer Relief Act of 2012. This established the federal exemption threshold at $5 million per individual, and a maximum tax rate of 40 percent above the exemption. The exemption is subject to indexing annually for inflation. For individuals who died in 2012, the exemption was $5.12 million; in 2013, it was $5.25 million; and in 2014, $5.34 million.

According to the Urban-Brookings Tax Policy Center, only 1.4 out of every 1,000 estates (0.14 percent) owed any tax in 2013. The Tax Policy Center's research reported in 2013 that 99.86 percent of estates owed no federal estate tax and that among the 3,780 estates that paid tax, the "effective" tax rate—that is, the percentage of the estate's value on which taxes were paid—averaged 16.6 percent.

All properties left to tax-exempt charities are not subject to federal estate tax. All property left to a surviving spouse passes free of federal estate tax. With the U.S. Supreme Court's 2013 decision (United States v. Windsor) this provision is now applicable to validly married same-sex couples. (The marital deduction is not applicable to property left to noncitizen spouses, but the personal tax exemption can be used for property left to noncitizen spouses.)

The American Taxpayer Relief Act of 2012 made permanent the "portability" of a deceased spouse's unused federal estate-tax exclusion. The provision was initially enacted as part of the Tax Relief, Unemployment Reauthorization, and Job Creation Act of 2010, effective for married persons dying on or after January 1, 2011, and would have ended December 31, 2012, had it not been made permanent by the ATRA of 2012.

Portability allows a surviving spouse to use a deceased spouse's unused estate-tax exclusion. In practical terms, for married persons dying in 2011 or later, if a first-to-die spouse has not fully used the federal estate-tax exclusion, the unused portion (known as the Deceased Spousal Unused Exclusion Amount) can be transferred or "ported" to the surviving spouse. For both federal gift and estate-tax purposes, the surviving spouse's exclusion is the sum of his/her own exclusion plus the first-to-die's ported DSUE amount. Using portability it is effectively possible to qualify and use the maximum total exemption, if the first to die has not used any of his/her federal gift-tax exemption. For example: A husband, John, and wife, Mary, are both U.S. citizens. John owns property valued at $5.34 million and Mary owns property valued at $5.34 million. John dies in 2014, leaving his entire $5.34 million estate to Mary, and has not used any of his federal estate-tax exemption. Since all of John's assets were transferred to Mary, his spouse, Mary's exemption in 2014 (for gift and/or estate-tax purposes) is $10.68 million. Mary could make gifts up to $10.68 million in 2014 and fully shield her estate from federal estate taxes.

In order for the surviving spouse to be able to use the DSUE amount, the executor of the first-to-die's estate must make the election on IRS Form 706, the same form that is required for estates exceeding the federal estate-tax exemption, and file it in a timely manner.

For estates with a gross value large enough to require the filing of a Federal Estate Tax return (IRS Form 706), the return (including an itemized appraisal) must be filed within nine months of the date of death. (If good cause can be shown, extensions of various lengths are available to file the return or to pay the tax, but interest accrues. Penalties may be assessed against the estate if the federal estate tax is not paid when due and extensions are not obtained.)

Federal law also requires an executor to submit an appraisal of assets, even if no federal estate taxes are due. The appraisal must be conducted within nine months of the date of death, with values to be determined as of the date of death at "fair market" value. Fair market value is defined by the IRS as the "the price that property would sell for on the open market. It is the price that would be agreed on between a willing buyer and a willing seller, with neither being required to act, and both having reasonable knowledge of the relevant facts."

Expert appraisals are suggested for tangible property, such as works of art, jewelry, precious metals, or coin and stamp collections. The IRS requires a professional appraisal if any one item is valued at more than $3,000, or any collection of items is valued at more than $10,000.

If your estate will be large enough to trigger federal estate tax, you should obtain advice from an experienced estate-planning professional who can help you sort through your options. There are a number of estate-planning tools you can use to reduce estate-tax liability.

FEDERAL ANNUAL GIFT-TAX EXCLUSION

In 2014 one could give up to $14,000 to any individual and $14,000 to as many individuals as desired without triggering the federal gift tax. (The allowable amount is indexed for inflation, so it is subject to change.)

In addition to gifts to individuals, one can give to qualified charities, a spouse, or a qualified political organization. An unlimited amount can be gifted to pay educational expenses—tuition—as long as the payment is made directly to the educational institution. Gifts used to pay for medical expenses are also unlimited, as long as payment is made to the medical facility.

Unified Credit

The federal estate tax and gift tax are integrated into one unified tax system. If a person exceeds the annual federal gift-tax exclusion amount in any year, he or she can pay the tax on the excess or take advantage of the unified credit to avoid paying the tax. The unified credit enables one to give away $5 million (plus the annual inflation adjustments, which was $5.34 million in 2014) during one's lifetime without having to pay gift tax. Use of the unified credit during one's lifetime reduces the amount available to offset federal estate tax upon death. However, if the gift tax is paid during life, the taxed gifts are added back to one's estate at death. Thus, the estate tax is recalculated, allowing the gift taxes previously paid to be credited against any final estate tax due.

Generation-skipping Transfer (GST) Tax Exemption

There are many types of trusts that can be used for estate planning. Because of the complexities involved in trusts, you should consult an estate-planning professional, an attorney specializing in taxes, or an accountant to learn about the advantages and possible disadvantages of establishing a trust.

Because many collectors desire to leave their numismatic collections—especially those of great value, or numismatic holdings that constitute the greatest portion of value in the estate—to children and grandchildren, it may be worth checking into what is sometimes referred to as a "dynasty trust" or generation-skipping trust in order to use the GST tax exemption, which in 2014 was $5.34 million. (The GST tax exemption is indexed for inflation, thus the amount is likely to change in the future.)

Individuals who might otherwise leave their entire estates outright to their children elect to use the generation-skipping exemption within an unlimited generation-skipping trust to benefit their children and grandchildren. Such trusts can be funded with cash or property (including numismatic holdings) worth up to the available generation-skipping transfer tax exemption. The generation-skipping tax exemption offers two important advantages:

1. The trust escapes all transfer taxes when children die and passes tax-free to grandchildren.
2. The trust is protected from the claims of creditors and, to some degree, from claims of ex-spouses. (If property in the trust had been left to children outright, it could be subject to such claims.)

STATE "DEATH" TAXES

Many people think all "death taxes" are the same. That is, they use the terms "estate tax" and "inheritance tax" interchangeably, believing they are the same. However, these are different and they are not interchangeable. In fact, two states (Maryland and New Jersey) collect both an estate tax and an inheritance tax.

Estate Tax

Estate tax (whether federal or state) is based on the net value of property owned by the deceased. The tax, if any is due, is paid by the estate and must be filed and paid before the estate can be closed or property transferred to the beneficiaries. Estate tax has nothing to do with the person who inherits property.

The good news is that the trend over the last decade among states has been to abolish state estate taxes. Currently only the District of Columbia and 14 states collect estate taxes. All states that collect estate taxes and the District of Columbia have exemptions, meaning that estates valued below a certain threshold are not taxed. The exemptions vary as do the rates applied to values above the established exemption.

Inheritance Tax

Inheritance tax is usually mandated and collected by state governments, although in at least one state (Nebraska) rates are set and collected by counties and administered locally. Currently inheritance taxes are collected in seven states. Inheritance tax rates vary widely depending on the person inheriting the property and his or her kinship to the deceased. In some states spouses are exempt from paying inheritance tax. In a number of states lineal heirs are exempt or pay a lesser amount of inheritance tax. Some states distinguish lineal descendants (children, grandchildren, great-grandchildren) and lineal ascendants (living predecessors, including parents, grandparents, great-grandparents). Some states now include exemptions for civil-union partners. Rates can also vary, depending on the value of the property inherited. For example, New Jersey has graduated rates from 11 to 16 percent on property valued above $500. There is no New Jersey inheritance tax imposed upon parents, grandparents, children and their descendants, spouses, civil-union partners, domestic partners or charities. New Jersey provides a $25,000 exemption for siblings, sons-in-law, and daughters-in-law.

Check the chart and notes provided. Identified are the District of Columbia and the 14 states (as of April 2014) that collect estate taxes as well as the seven states that collect inheritance taxes. The notes provide brief details about exemptions and rates.

If you do not live in these states or the District of Columbia, you probably will not have to worry about estate taxes or inheritance taxes for your estate. However, it is entirely possible that you may inherit property from someone who had legal residence in one of the states or the District of Columbia at the time of his or her death. Also, be sure to check from time to time the status of the state in which you reside. Tax laws can be changed quickly through legislation signed into law.

Estate and Inheritance Taxes: States and District of Columbia
Information current as of April 2014.

State	Estate	Inheritance	State	Estate	Inheritance
Connecticut	Yes	No	Minnesota	Yes	No
Delaware	Yes	No	Nebraska	No	Yes
D.C.	Yes	No	New Jersey	Yes	Yes
Hawaii	Yes	No	New York	Yes	No
Illinois	Yes	No	Oregon	Yes	No
Iowa	No	Yes	Pennsylvania	No	Yes
Kentucky	No	Yes	Rhode Island	Yes	No
Maine	Yes	No	Tennessee*	No	Yes
Maryland	Yes	Yes	Vermont	Yes	No
Massachusetts	Yes	No	Washington	Yes	No

* Although defined as inheritance tax, value is based on property; see page 243.

Connecticut Estate Tax: Progressive rate of 7.2% for estates valued at $2 million and higher; 12% maximum above $10.1 million.

Delaware Estate Tax: $5.25 million exemption; maximum rate 16%.

District of Columbia Estate Tax: Estates valued at more than $1 million taxed; maximum rate is 16%.

Hawaii Estate Tax: Estates below $3.6 million exempt. Tax rates range from less than 1 to a maximum of 16%.

Illinois Estate Tax: $4 million exemption beginning in 2013. Maximum rate is 16%.

Iowa Inheritance Tax: Rate ranges up to maximum of 15% for estates valued at $25,000 or more. No taxes for surviving spouse, stepchildren, lineal descendants, or lineal ascendants.

Kentucky Inheritance Tax: Spouse, parent, child, grandchild, siblings exempt. Other beneficiaries subject to tax, ranging from 4 to 16%.

Maine Estate Tax: $2 million exemption; above $2 million rate ranges from 8 to 12%.

Maryland Estate Tax: Estates exceeding $1 million taxed; maximum rate is 16%. **Maryland Inheritance Tax:** Property passed to individuals other than spouse, lineal descendants, lineal ascendants, sibling, or spouse of child is taxed at 10%.

Massachusetts Estate Tax: Below $1 million exempt; ranges from 0.8% for $1 million to 16% for estates exceeding $10,040,000.

Minnesota Estate Tax: $1 million exemption. Maximum rate is 16%.

Nebraska Inheritance Tax: Local tax administered by counties; ranges from 1 to 18%. Spouse and charities exempt.

New Jersey Estate Tax: Estates exceeding $675,000 not passing to spouse or civil-union partner taxed; 16 % maximum tax. **New Jersey Inheritance Tax:** Graduated rates from 11 to 16% on property valued above $500. No tax for parents, grandparents, descendants, children and their descendants, spouses, civil-union partners, domestic partners, or charities. $25,000 exemption for siblings, sons-in-law, and daughters-in-law.

New York Estate Tax: Estates exceeding $1 million; ranges to maximum of 16%.

Oregon Estate Tax: Up to $1 million exempt. Rates range from 10 to 16% for $1 million up to $9.5 million. Maximum rate is 16%.

Pennsylvania Inheritance Tax: 4.5% for lineal heirs, 12% for siblings, 15% for other heirs (except charitable organizations, exempt institutions, government entities).

Rhode Island Estate Tax: $910,725 exemption for 2013; adjusted each January for inflation. Maximum rate of 16%.

Tennessee Inheritance Tax: State defines tax as an inheritance tax. However, law taxes property instead of heirs. Based on value exceeding $2 million exemption in 2014 and $5 million exemption in 2015; rate ranges from 5.5 to 9.5%. Inheritance tax to be phased out as of January 1, 2016.

CAPITAL GAINS AND LOSSES— COLLECTIBLES

As indicated earlier, values declared on the final inventory or appraisal have real consequences for the person who inherits coins or other numismatic collectibles via an estate or trust, because the value listed in these legal documents becomes the "basis value" for computing capital-gains tax when the person who received the coin(s) sells it.

For tax purposes, *collectibles* refers to personal property that is easily portable and includes coins, stamps, precious metals, precious gems, rare rugs, antiques, alcoholic beverages, and fine art. Precious-metal bullion coins produced by government mints in nations such as Austria, Australia, Canada, Great Britain, and South Africa are taxed at the same capital-gains rate as bullion coins produced in the United States (such as the U.S. Mint's gold, silver, and platinum American Eagles). The same applies to Gold ETFs (exchange traded funds) and Silver ETFs. (Certain precious-metal bullion coins approved by the IRS for inclusion in self-directed Individual Retirement Accounts are considered regular investment assets and are not defined as collectibles for tax purposes under Section 408[m][3] of the Internal Revenue Code. Consult with your tax adviser for current, applicable laws on these items.)

Many people are under the impression that it is best to "lowball" values so as to avoid estate or inheritance taxes. Exactly the *opposite* is true with regard to capital gains. It is important to determine current fair market value for numismatic items in an estate or trust that will be distributed because the value assigned will become the "basis value" for the person who inherits or receives them. The basis value will have capital gains (or loss) implications when the heir sells the coins(s) or other numismatic items.

Collectibles are taxed in two different capital-gains tax brackets:

Short-term collectible capital-gains rate: Collectibles held for *less than one year* are currently taxed at one's personal income-tax rate.

Long-term collectible capital-gains rate: Collectibles held for *one year or longer* are currently taxed at 28%.

Bullion coins, such as these Austrian Vienna Philharmonic gold and silver pieces, are taxed at the same capital-gains rate as numismatic coins.

In illustrating the differences and ramifications of basis declaration, we will use as an example a person who inherited a $20 gold Saint-Gaudens double eagle via his uncle's estate, created on the date his uncle died in 2013. The heir keeps the coin for more than one year after receiving it and then decides to sell it. (Costs for storage and auction fees could be added to increase the basis value, but to keep the math simple, we are assuming no other value was added to the basis for our three scenarios.)

Value could have been listed on the final inventory as $20, which is the face value. Or, the coin could have been valued as "bullion." With gold trading at $1,300.00 an ounce, it would have had a current market value of $1,170.00 (because the coin is comprised of 90 percent gold). Through an independent appraisal the coin was identified as a 1920-S Saint-Gaudens double eagle, graded MS-63, with a current fair market value in 2013 of $115,000.

Case study: You inherit a Mint State 1920-S double eagle. What value should you assign it, for tax purposes?

What are the consequences of these valuations for the person who received this coin from the estate?

Scenario A: The value of the gold coin is declared to be $20, its face value. The person who inherited the coin decides to sell the coin more than a year later, learns of its numismatic value, and to his great surprise sells it for $150,000. He would be subject to capital gains tax on $149,980. Basis value for the coin was $20, thus $150,000 - $20 = $149,980 capital gains × 28%. *Capital-gains tax would be $41,994.40.*

Scenario B: The value of the gold coin is declared to be $1,170.00., the value of the gold in the coin on the date of death of the person in whose estate the coin resided. The person who inherited the coin decides to sell the coin more than a year after inheriting it, learns of its numismatic value, and to his great surprise sells it for $150,000. The basis value for the coin was $1,170.00, thus $150,000 - $1,170.00 = $148,830.00 capital gains × 28%. *Capital-gains tax would be $41,672.40.*

Scenario C: The numismatic value of the gold coin is declared to be $115,000 via an independent appraisal for the 90-day inventory. The person who inherited the coin decides to sell the coin more than a year after inheriting it and receives $150,000 for it. Basis value for the coin was $115,000, thus $150,000 - $115,000 = $35,000 capital gains × 28%. *Capital-gains tax would be $9,800.*

So how much, after taxes, would the person actually realize under each scenario?

A: $150,000 - $41,994.40 = $108,005.60

B: $150,000 - $41,672.40 = $108,327.60

C: $150,000 - $9,800.00 = $140,200.00

Obviously, scenario C is the best. Whether you are the executor of an estate or an heir, the benefits of an independent appraisal are obvious.

Generally speaking, assets that tend to increase in value over time (coins and other numismatic collectibles, for example) should be identified as property in the estate because, if administered through an estate, the heir benefits from the step-up in basis. (A coin or other property is valued at the fair market value at the time of inheritance, not at the value at which the deceased purchased it.)

Let's also consider an example of a capital loss. We will use as an example a generic circulation-strike 2012 American Gold Eagle coin containing one ounce of gold. On the date of the uncle's death in 2013, the coin was valued at $1,300, based on the world market price of gold. A value of $1,300 for the coin was listed in the estate's final inventory. The person who inherited the coin held it for more than one year and sold it for $1,150, which constituted a capital loss of $150 ($1,300 - $1,150 = $150). Any loss up to $3,000 can be subtracted from capital gains or declared as a loss against ordinary income. Under current tax statutes, losses of more than $3,000 can be carried forward to offset future years' taxable income. No more than $3,000 can be deducted in any tax year against ordinary income. (Consult your tax adviser and be aware that tax treatment of losses may change.)

American Taxpayer Relief Act of 2012: Rate Changes

Legislation approved by Congress and signed into law by President Barack Obama at the end of 2012 set rates that apply to the short-term collectible capital gains. Recall that gains from *collectibles held for less than one year* are taxed at one's personal income-tax rate. For those with taxable income below certain levels, tax rates remain at 10%, 15%, 25%, 28%, 33% and 35%. For a single person with taxable income above $400,000, married couples filing jointly with taxable income over $450,000, a married person filing separately with taxable income over $225,000, and heads of household with taxable income over $425,000, the rate is 39.6%.

The American Taxpayer Relief Act of 2012 also made changes in "regular" capital gains, that is, capital gains applicable to investments other than collectibles. Again, the change affected those in the higher taxable income levels ($400,000; $450,000; $225,000; or $425,000) by increasing their capital-gains tax from 15 to 20%. For those in the lower taxable-income brackets, the capital-gains rate remains 15%.

The Health Care and Education Reconciliation Act of 2010

The Health Care and Education Reconciliation Act of 2010 (also known as ObamaCare) imposes a 3.8% tax. It is the Net Investment Income Tax (NIIT), which is sometimes referred to as the Medicare surtax. NIIT applies to certain individuals, estates, and trusts that have income above statutorily defined threshold amounts effective for tax years beginning after December 31, 2013. (It did not affect income-tax returns for the 2012 taxable year filed in 2013.) This 3.8% additional tax is levied on net investment income, which is income from interest, dividends, tax-exempt bond interest, royalties, rents, capital gains, etc.

Estates and Trusts

Estates and trusts are subject to the Net Investment Income Tax (NIIT) if they have undistributed net investment income and also have adjusted gross income over the dollar amount at which the highest tax bracket for an estate or trust begins for the taxable year. For tax year 2014, the estate and trust threshold amount was $12,150. (There are special computational rules for certain unique types of trusts, such a Charitable Remainder Trusts and Electing Small Business Trusts.) For threshold amounts for future years, check with the IRS or your tax preparer.

Individuals

The NIIT applies to persons with net investment income or the excess of individual's modified adjusted gross income over the threshold amount. The thresholds are $250,000 for a married couple filing jointly or a surviving spouse; $125,000 for a married person filing separately; and $200,000 for a single individual.

Again, let's draw from our earlier capital-gains examples. For this, we will use as an example a single heir who held the coin he inherited for more than a year and who has an adjusted taxable earned income of $100,000.

> **Scenario A:** The inherited coin was valued at face value of $20, and sold for $150,000. Capital gains were $149,980. Earned taxable income of $100,000 + $149,980 capital gains from sale of the coin = $249,980. His threshold amount is $200,000. So he must pay 3.8% NIIT on the $49,980, amounting to $1,899.24.

> **Scenario B:** The inherited coin was valued at $1,170, based on the price of gold on the date of death of the person in whose estate the coin resided, and it was sold for $150,000. Capital gains were $148,830. Earned taxable income of $100,000 + $148,830 capital gains from sale of the coin = $248,830. His threshold amount is $200,000. So he must pay 3.8% NIIT on the $48,830, amounting to $1,855.54.

> **Scenario C:** The numismatic value of the gold coin was declared to be $115,000 via an independent appraisal for the 90-day inventory. The coin was sold for $150,000. Capital gains were $35,000.

His threshold amount is $200,000. Earned taxable income of $100,000 + $35,000 capital gains from sale of the coin = $135,000. Since the $135,000 does not exceed the $200,000 threshold, he would not owe any NIIT as a result of selling the coin.

STATE SALES TAXES ON PRECIOUS METALS, COINS, AND BULLION BARS

Nineteen states and the District of Columbia (as of May 2014) collect state sales tax on coins and bars made of precious metals such as silver, gold, and platinum. The states include: Alabama, Arkansas, Hawaii, Indiana, Kansas, Kentucky, Maine, Minnesota, Mississippi, New Jersey, New Mexico, Nevada, North Carolina, Ohio, Tennessee, Vermont, Virginia, West Virginia, and Wisconsin. The rates vary. Often a local sales tax is added.

As this edition was going to press, bills were under consideration in Minnesota and Ohio seeking exemptions. It would be prudent to check with dealers within your state to ascertain the current status if you reside in a state that imposes sales tax.

During the past two decades the Industry Council for Tangible Assets (www.ictaonline.org) has worked with coin dealers and leaders in the numismatic community to obtain sales-tax exemptions that benefit dealers as well as collectors and investors.

Currently 19 states do not collect sales tax on precious metals, coins, and bullion: Alaska, Arizona, Colorado, Delaware, Idaho, Illinois, Iowa, Louisiana, Michigan, Missouri, Montana, North Dakota, Oregon, Pennsylvania, Rhode Island, South Carolina, South Dakota, Utah, and Washington. Four of these states (Louisiana, Missouri, Pennsylvania, and Rhode Island) collect tax on sales of paper money. Also, note that although these 19 states do not collect sales tax on precious metals, coins, and bullion, some states tax non-coin numismatic collectibles (such as tokens and medals), and some cities within these states impose a local sales tax.

The remaining 12 states have varying types of exemptions, primarily based on the amount of the sale. For example, purchases with a total value of $1,000 or more may be exempt, whereas coins or bars valued below the exemption would be taxed.

The imposition of state and local sales taxes have forced many buyers to purchase most of their bullion coins via the Internet, especially small numbers of such coins that do not meet minimum exemptions.

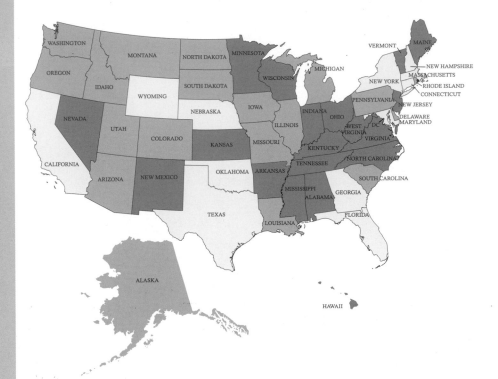

Red = Does collect tax (Alabama, Arkansas, Hawaii, Indiana, Kansas, Kentucky, Maine, Minnesota, Mississippi, New Jersey, New Mexico, Nevada, North Carolina, Ohio, Tennessee, Vermont, Virginia, West Virginia, and Wisconsin)

Green = Does not collect tax (Alaska, Arizona, Colorado, Delaware, Idaho, Illinois, Iowa, Louisiana, Michigan, Missouri, Montana, North Dakota, Oregon, Pennsylvania, Rhode Island, South Carolina, South Dakota, Utah, and Washington)

Yellow = Has exemptions

U.S. FEDERAL REPORTING LAWS
Cash Reporting

Coin dealers or merchants who receive a cash payment of more than $10,000 for a single transaction or a series of related transactions are required to file a Federal Form 8300 reporting the transaction. The IRS defines the term "cash" as currency (U.S. or foreign) and bearer instruments such as cashier's checks, money orders, traveler's checks, and other instruments if the face value is less than $10,000. Certain paper-money collections may also qualify.

Collectors and investors should be aware of these federal reporting requirements for dealers. Do not ask a dealer to waive reporting, because you would be asking the person to violate U.S. laws. Violations carry stiff fines and penalties.

Broker Reporting

If you pay cash when buying large amounts of gold Canadian Maple Leaf, South African Krugerrand, or Mexican Onza gold coins; silver, gold, or platinum bars in volume; or $1,000 or more in face value of 90 percent silver U.S. coins (any combination of dimes, quarters, half dollars), the merchant from whom you purchase is required to file a Form 1099-B.

Federal Form 1099-B Reportable Items

REPORTABLE ITEMS	FINENESS	MINIMUM AMOUNT
Coins		
Gold Maple Leaf	0.9999	25 1-oz. coins
Gold Krugerrand	0.9167	25 1-oz. coins
Gold Mexican Onza	0.9000	25 1-oz. coins
Silver U.S. coins (10, 25, 50 cents)	0.9000	Any combination totaling $1,000 face value
Bars		
Silver	0.9990	Any size totaling 1,000 troy oz. or more
Gold	0.9950	Any size totaling 1 kg (32.14 troy oz.) or more
Platinum	0.9995	Any size totaling 25 troy oz. or more
Palladium	0.9995	Any size totaling 100 troy oz. or more

Key terms and phrases you need to know and understand before you talk to potential buyers. Knowing them won't make you an expert, but being able to talk and understand the lingo will keep you from being perceived as a novice.

13

TALKING THE TALK

E ach specialized area of endeavor has its own jargon and nomenclature. So does the world of money, especially the collecting sector. In reading this book and learning how to identify and value your coins and other collectibles, you have encountered some of the need-to-know terms that will be useful in approaching possible buyers. Herein we will delve a little deeper into some of the terminology and introduce you to some other words that you are likely to encounter. The list is not a comprehensive glossary; rather, it is intended as a practical guide to help level the playing field and to help you approach your goal of selling your coins with confidence.

Tip #1: One of the most difficult words to master for most people new to the field is *numismatics*. While it is useful to know the definition—the science, study, and collecting of coins, tokens, medals, decorations, paper money, or any objects once used as money—do not feel compelled to use the word or its related terms in conversation. *Coin collecting, coin collector, coin* *dealer*, and *collector value* will do just fine. Better to use these terms than to stumble in pronunciations—a significant clue that you are new to the field. If you are fearless and determined to master the terms, use the pronunciation guides and practice until the words roll off your tongue without hesitation and effortlessly.

numismatics (noun)—nu-mis-mat-ics (pronounced *new-miz-MAT-icks*)—The study and/or collecting of money and any objects once used as money. Synonym: coin collecting.

numismatist (noun)—nu-mis-ma-tist (pronounced *new-MIZ-ma-tist*)— A person who studies or collects money. Synonym: coin collector.

professional numismatist (noun)—A business person who buys and sells coins and other numismatic collectibles. Synonym: coin dealer.

numismatic (adjective)—nu-mis-mat-ic (pronounced *new-miz-MAT-ick*)—Used to modify or describe related words. Examples: numismatic value, numismatic researcher, numismatic writer, American Numismatic Association. Numismatic value includes a coin's or note's collector premium above its face value or bullion value due to rarity and grade rarity.

American pronunciations of *numismatics* and *numismatist* are available at a number of sites on the Internet, including www.macmillandictionary .com/pronunciation/american/numismatics.

> **Tip #2:** Never approach a possible buyer by saying, "I don't know anything about these coins." Such proclamations are an invitation to be fleeced. If you have read and followed the recommendations in earlier chapters, you now have some knowledge about the coins and other numismatic collectibles you have and their value. And, you should be prepared to respond to the question you will be asked: "How much do you want for your coins?"

The following list contains words and terms you may encounter as you talk with possible buyers. It includes words already introduced in earlier chapters as well as some new words.

accumulation—Collectible objects such as coins, medals, tokens, paper money that are unsorted, unattributed, and unclassified.

alloy—A mixture or combination of two or more metals.

altered coin—A coin that has been intentionally changed to make it appear to be more valuable or rare. Examples of alteration include changing digits in dates, adding mintmarks, and moving metal to fill in weakly struck design devices.

ancient coin—In general, any coin made or issued before 500 A.D.

assay—A test performed to determine the fineness, weight, or consistency of metals used to make coins or bullion bars. May also refer to a piece on which the test has been conducted.

back—The reverse side of a piece of paper money. The side opposite the face.

base metal—A non-precious metal such as copper and zinc.

blank—A round disc or formed piece of metal that becomes a coin or medal when struck by dies.

bourse—The room or exhibit hall in which buying and selling of coins and numismatic items takes place during a coin show.

bronze—An alloy of copper, zinc, and tin.

Buffalo nickel—The name frequently used for the Indian Head five-cent coin.

bullion—Precious metals such as silver, gold, and platinum in the form of bars, ingots, plate and other items.

bullion coin—A coin made of silver, gold, or platinum, whose value is based on the world market price of the precious metal rather than the denomination or face value stated on the coin.

business strike—A coin struck for circulation without any special treatment or finishes. Also referred to as an Uncirculated coin or a circulation strike.

buyer's fee—A fee charged of the winning bidder by an auction house. Fees are usually a percentage of the amount paid for the item purchased. *Buyer's fee* is sometime referred to as *buyer premium*. The buyer's fee should be stated in the terms and conditions of the sale and published prior to the commencement of an auction.

cabinet friction—Wear imparted on the surface of a coin, token, or medal due to the friction between the object and the container in which it is housed, such as a tray or envelope.

clad coin—A coin made of copper-nickel or silver bonded to a core of pure copper; i.e., U.S. dimes, quarters, half dollars, and some dollars made since 1965. Dollar coins made since 2000 with copper, zinc, manganese, and nickel bonded to a core of pure copper.

certified coin—A coins that has been authenticated and graded by an independent, third-party professional coin-grading service and encased in a plastic holder.

cherrypicker—One with advanced knowledge who searches accumulations, collections, and dealers' stock to find rare and valuable coins.

coin—A piece of (usually) metal with special markings, including a designation of value, issued by a governmental authority for use as money.

commemorative—A coin, medal, token, or paper note issued to honor a person, place, or event. Commemorative coins and notes are made for circulation as well as for the non-circulating collector market.

contact marks—Minor marks on the surface of an Uncirculated coin, obtained by the coin colliding with others in bins and bags during the manufacturing and distribution process.

crack-out—A coin or piece of paper money that has been removed from a professional grading service holder for the purpose of resubmitting in order to obtain a higher grade.

counterfeit—An exact or nearly exact replica coin, note, or other object intended to deceive or defraud.

currency—Legal tender. *Currency* applies to both coins and paper money. Some people use the word in reference only to paper money.

die—A metal punch engraved with incused mirror-image markings and a design that imparts the image when impressed into a coin blank or planchet. Separate dies are used for the obverse and reverse of a coin or medal.

die variety—A coin struck from dies that are normal except for minor design variations; for example, slight changes in the location of digits, letters, stars, or other design elements unique to a particular die of a design series.

dollar—A unit of coined and paper money in the United States and many other countries.

double eagle—A $20 U.S. gold coin.

doubled die—A double or multiple image of a design element created during the die-manufacturing process. Coins struck by a doubled die are called *doubled die coins*, with descriptors noting the area of the coin that exhibits the doubled image (e.g., *doubled die obverse; doubled LIBERTY*).

eagle—A denomination of U.S. gold coins; also the $10 gold coin.

edge—The surface of a coin perpendicular to the obverse and reverse.

encapsulated coin—A coin that has been sonically sealed in a plastic holder, usually by a third-party grading service. Also called a *slabbed coin*.

error—A coin, paper note, token, or medal that exhibits a mistake made during its manufacture; e.g., being struck off-center, or with a clipped planchet.

exergue—(pronounced *ex-urg*)—The area on a coin below the main design element, often where the date is located.

exonumia—(pronounced *ex-o-NOOM-ia*)—A category of numismatic collectibles including tokens, medals, badges, etc., that do not have legal-tender status.

eye appeal—Aesthetic appeal of a coin, or its overall attractiveness, as judged by the one viewing it. Eye appeal is the most subjective factor in determining the grade of a coin.

face—The front side of a piece of paper money, opposite the back.

face value—The denomination and value stated on a coin or piece of paper money.

field—The flat surface of a coin surrounding raised design elements.

fineness—The purity of precious metal expressed in terms of one thousand parts. For example: 90 percent silver is .900 fine.

flip—A holder for coins containing two pockets—one for the coin, one for an insert containing information about the coin. The name is derived from folding over or "flipping" the holder to close it in order to prevent the coin from escaping.

grading—The process of determining the state of preservation of a numismatic collectible.

hairlines—Tiny, fine scratches on the surface of a coin, caused by wiping with a cloth.

half eagle—A $5 gold U.S. coin.

hammer price—The price an auctioneer calls when an item is sold. It does not include any associated fees such as a buyer's fee or a seller's fee.

hobo nickel—An Indian Head five-cent coin that has been carved so the Indian Head resembles a hobo or other character. The bison on the reverse sometimes is also carved to resemble a person, a donkey, or some other figure.

hub—A positive-image punch used to impress a coin's design into a die for coinage.

incuse—An adjective describing a design element below the surface of a coin, token, or medal.

inscription—Lettering or a legend that appears on a coin, medal, or token.

intrinsic value—The melt value of the precious metal contained in a coin.

investment grade—An adjective describing a coin graded Mint State– 65 or above purchased primarily for investment.

junk silver—Pre-1965 circulated 90 percent silver dimes, quarters, half dollars, and dollars (and 40 percent silver half dollars of 1965–1969) that are valuable for their silver content but do not carry a premium due to their numismatic value.

key coin—The rarest or most valuable coin of a specific denomination or design series; e.g., the 1916-D Winged Liberty dime.

large cent—A U.S. one-cent coin minted from 1793 through 1857. Their diameters range from 26 to 29 millimeters, compared to the modern small cent's 19 mm.

legal tender—Coins and paper money designated by a government that can be used in the discharge of debt.

legal tender bullion coin—A coin made of precious metal, produced and sold by a government mint for the investment market. These do not circulate as money, but have legal tender status and have a nominal face value stated on them. Bullion coins trade in world markets based on the value of the precious metals they contain.

legend—An inscription on a coin, medal, token, or other numismatic item.

lettered edge—Incused or raised letters on the edge of a coin.

luster—The surface quality of a coin created by light reflecting from microscopic flow lines in the metal.

medal—A disc, usually of metal, bearing a design and inscriptions, struck to honor a person, place, or event or for artistic purposes. A medal is not denominated and is not intended for use as money.

medallion—A large medal, usually three inches in diameter or larger. Also, a large Roman presentation piece dating from the fifth century.

medieval coin—A coin struck from 500 to 1500 A.D.

Mercury dime—The name sometimes used for the Winged Liberty Head dime produced from 1916 through 1945. Shorty after its issue, some people mistook the female Head of Liberty, wearing a winged cap, for the Greek male god Mercury.

mintmark—A small letter or symbol identifying the minting facility that produced a particular coin.

Mint set—A set of Uncirculated coins struck, packaged, and sold by a government mint, which includes one of each coin produced by each minting facility for circulation during the year.

modern coin—In general, any coin minted after 1500 A.D. Among U.S. coins, *modern* usually refers to those struck beginning in the mid-1960s, when the U.S. Mint changed from 90 percent silver to clad coinage.

motto—A word or phrase inscribed on a coin, medal, or token.

mule—A coin, medal, or token struck using two dies that are not normally or officially used in striking the design or denomination.

nickel—A white metal, silvery in color, used in coinage and often alloyed with copper. Also a nickname used for one-cent, three-cent, and five-cent coins made of a nickel alloy.

noncirculating legal tender coin—A coin made for sale to collectors, which does not circulate but has legal tender status in its country of origin. Abbreviated NCLT.

numismatics—The science, study, and collecting of money or any objects once used as money.

numismatist—One highly knowledgeable in numismatics.

obverse—The front side of a coin, medal, or token. Commonly called the "heads" side because it often depicts a portrait.

overdate—A die variety created by one or more numerals being superimposed over the date of a previously dated die. Can also occur in the manufacturing process when two hubs of different dates are used to make a die.

overmintmark—A die variety created when a mintmark for one minting facility is punched over the mintmark of another facility.

patina—Coloration on the surface of coin, medal, or token, caused by oxidation, generally over a long period of time.

penny—A denomination of British and Commonwealth coinage. *Penny* is commonly used in the United States as a nickname for the one-cent coin.

planchet—A blank metal disc that has been prepared for coinage and is ready to be struck into a coin.

Proof—A coin made by using specially prepared planchets, dies, and coining presses. Proof coins are usually struck at least twice. They represent the highest-quality coin produced.

proof—In the manufacture of paper money, a print made to test the quality and correctness of the plate.

prooflike—An Uncirculated coin struck from dies that have been specially prepared to create mirror surfaces on the coin.

Proof set—A set produced, packaged, and sold by a government mint, that contains Proof versions of the coin denominations struck for circulation during a given year.

quarter eagle—U.S. $2.50 gold coin.

raw coin—A coin that has not been encapsulated or "slabbed" by a third-party grading service.

relief—Design devices raised from the flat surface of a coin, medal, or token.

replica—A copy or reproduction of a numismatic item. All copies produced or sold in the United States since 1973 are required by law to have the word COPY incused on at least one side.

reverse—The back side of a coin, token, or medal. Often called the "tails" side.

rim—The raised part of a coin, around its circumference. Different from the edge.

seal—A device printed on U.S. paper money indicating its authority of issue. Current Federal Reserve Notes bear two seals: a green Department of the Treasury seal and a black Federal Reserve seal.

seller's fee—A fee charged by an auction house of the person who consigns a coin or numismatic item for sale. The seller's fee is usually a percentage of the hammer price or selling price called by the auctioneer at the time of final sale. Sometimes referred to as the *seller's premium*. The seller's fee should be stated in the terms and conditions of the sale and published prior to the commencement of an auction. Depending on the size and importance of items consigned, many auction houses will negotiate the percentage for the seller's fee.

serial number—In U.S. paper money, a number used to indicate order of production. Also, used as an anti-counterfeiting device.

series—Coins of the same denomination, design, and type.

series date—On the face of U.S. paper money, a major design change or year when a new secretary of the Treasury is confirmed.

slab—Nickname for a hard plastic case used by professional grading services to encapsulate authenticated and graded coins.

spot price—The market price of a precious metal traded daily and quoted on major exchanges.

sterling silver—Silver that is .925 fine.

token—A privately issued disc or item made of durable goods (e.g., metal or plastic) for use as a substitute for money and typically used in exchange of goods and services. Also sometimes used as an advertising piece.

type—A series of coins or notes distinguished by shared design, denomination, or composition.

type set—A collection of coins or paper money containing one each of a given series or period.

Uncirculated coin—A coin struck for circulation that exhibits no wear and displays original surfaces and luster. Also called *Mint State*.

unique—Only one specimen known.

variety—A design variation distinctive from the original of the type.

vignette—A pictorial element on paper money. Vignettes usually shade off into the surrounding unprinted or background area.

wheaties—Nickname for Lincoln cents with the Wheat Ears reverse, issued from 1909 through 1958.

whizzing—Severe polishing done to superficially improve the appearance of a coin. Whizzing is considered a deceptive practice and it lowers the value of a coin.

wooden nickel—A round or rectangular piece of wood, historically produced in many denominations and used as a money substitute during the Great Depression (1931 to 1934). Today wooden nickels are produced principally as souvenirs and advertising items.

year set—A privately packaged set containing one coin of each denomination produced for circulation from each minting facility during a given year.

zinc—A base metal used in many coinage alloys worldwide. Zinc's most prominent use in the United States is in the Lincoln cent produced for circulation since 1982, which is 97.5 percent zinc plated with a microscopic layer of copper.

14

FINDING
A BUYER

Finding the best buyer for your coins or collectibles with numismatic value is one of the most important aspects of your undertaking. In creating your inventory, you have identified your coins, estimated grades and values, and under some circumstances may have had reason to seek an independent appraisal of your holdings.

As you have undertaken this journey, you may have decided that you want to *keep* the coins and other items you have. It might be possible to use them as a core for expanding your collection. If so, you have learned the value of keeping an up-to-date inventory and how to properly handle and store your coins. The world of coin collecting offers many opportunities. A good place to start the next phase of your collecting journey is joining a local coin club or a national one such as the American Numismatic Association. Check the ANA's web site, www.money.org, for information, and subscribe to numismatic publications such as *Coin World* (www.coinworld.com) and *Numismatic*

There are many possible buyers for your coins. The key is finding the best buyer or the one who will pay you fair market value. Explore the many options open to you as a seller.

News (www.numismaticnews.net) to learn more about collecting, upcoming shows, and events that abound in educational activities where you can learn and meet people who share your collecting interests. You may also find new collecting areas.

If your intent is to sell your coins, there are a number of considerations to explore. What you have discovered in creating your inventory will help guide you to the best buyers.

COIN DEALERS

Most coin dealers buy and sell a wide range of coins and numismatic collectibles, so they would be likely candidates to purchase the coins you have for sale, especially those that carry a numismatic premium. Coin dealers buy as close to wholesale as possible and sell close to retail or above. They earn their living by buying and selling coins. The difference between wholesale and retail for a coin dealer is not all profit. A coin dealer (like other small-business owners) must cover costs of doing business (rent or payments on the building, utilities, bourse fees, insurance, travel, salaries, taxes, etc.) before getting to profit. Also, a coin dealer must consider the costs of holding a coin in inventory. Common-date and lower-grade coins (those with minimal numismatic value) tend to have the highest spreads between wholesale and retail because they are "slow movers." In general, expect a coin dealer to offer from 50 to 75 percent of retail value, especially if you have just a few common-date coins. If you have what are termed "better dates" (semi-key or key dates within a popularly collected design series) in higher grade ranges, a dealer will likely pay 80 to 90 percent of retail, depending on his "need" for the particular series. If a dealer has a ready customer in mind, chances are he will be willing to pay more. Many coin dealers work closely with their collector clients and are aware of the various coins on their customers' want lists. Some coin dealers specialize in a particular series, or in high-end coins (rare and high-grade pieces).

There are local brick-and-mortar coin shops (that is to say, with an actual physical address, not just a web site or mailbox) in most towns and cities throughout the United States. Some are relatively small; others are large businesses. The advantage of a brick-and-mortar shop is that it is a traditional business that deals with its customers face to face in an office or store that the business owns or rents. You can visit the shop, get an understanding of the types of coins and other collectibles they buy and sell, and not feel pressured that you have to make a snap decision when selling. Local coin shops often have specialists on staff who can help you identify coins that you may not have been able to find in

After you create an inventory of your coins, a professional coin dealer can make an offer to buy.

the Red Book or other resources mentioned herein. If you have key dates or other rarities that are likely candidates for grading by an independent third-party grading service, a local coin dealer may be able to assist you in that process, if the business is an authorized dealer for third-party grading services.

Regardless of the size of the coin dealership, it is important to do your homework. Know with whom you are about to deal before you attempt to transact business. Check with the Better Business Bureau to learn whether there are any outstanding complaints. Also, check as to whether the owners or staff are members in good standing of organizations such as the American Numismatic Association or the Professional Numismatists Guild. Dealer members of these organizations are required to follow a code of ethics and both organizations offer a process for resolving complaints when disputes arise. Both organizations have web sites where you can search for dealer members by state, city, or zip code to find those near you.

ANA: www.money.org/membership/dealer-directory.aspx

PNG: www.pngdealers.com/dealersearch.php

These directories list contact information as well as the specialties and types of coins / numismatic collectibles each dealer buys and sells.

It is also possible to find coin dealers by using computer search engines such as Google. Type in "coin dealer" and the name of your city or locality and click "Search." You will find listings as well as web sites. Perform the same due diligence regarding dealers listed online as with a brick-and-mortar location. Most traditional coin shops today also have web sites. If you visit a dealer's web site, check on the home page. If the firm or its principals are members of numismatic organizations such as the ANA and PNG, you will usually find membership logos displayed at the bottom of the page. You may also see the logo of ICTA, the Industry Council for Tangible Assets, which is a trade organization for precious-metals dealers. Many coin dealers are members of ICTA because they buy and sell bullion coins. Most good web sites have a section titled "About Us." Be sure to click "About Us" to read about the business and profiles of the owners and staff. If the principals of the business are members of numismatic organizations, they usually are prominently listed.

There are some do's and don'ts when selecting and meeting with coin dealers.

- Do check the credentials of the coin dealer or firm with whom you are considering doing business.
- Do identify the type of coins / numismatic collectibles the dealer buys and sells.
- Do call or send an email inquiry to make an appointment to meet with the dealer or a member of his staff regarding coins you have for sale.
- Do, if you have a small number of coins, be prepared to transport them to the coin shop, using an inconspicuous briefcase or boxes that will adequately protect them.
- Do, if you have a large number of coins, select a few representative examples. Take the samples and a copy of your inventory list with you for your first meeting with the dealer. If the dealer is interested in purchasing or viewing all of the coins, set up a second appointment. It is best if you can transport all of the coins to the dealer's shop. If that is not possible, arrange for the dealer to view your coins in a private room at your bank or the storage facility in which you keep the coins. If you keep your coins in your home and are unable to take them to the coin shop, arrange to take your coins and meet with the dealer in a secure, public place. Check with your bank, savings and loan, or credit union for possible use of a conference room. If none is available, check with your attorney or a friend who has a business that may have a conference room that would provide a high level of security and privacy.

- Do, if possible, select up to three coin dealers to view your coins, and from whom to obtain bids.

- Do get the dealer's offer in writing, including an itemized list of coins he will purchase and prices he is willing to pay.

- Don't sell your coins to jewelers, pawn shops, or entities that set up during the weekend at a local motel to buy coins and precious metals. Although some may be knowledgeable about some coins, most jewelers and pawn shops are not readily familiar with coins of numismatic value. They rarely offer more than bullion value. Undercover investigations have shown that the transient buyers who set up in motels during weekends sometimes are not licensed to do business in the area or state and may not be operating with certified equipment, such as scales that weigh accurately. Also, transient buyers frequently are reluctant to provide a written bill of sale, itemizing purchases.

- Don't set up appointments with strangers to come into your home to view coins.

Dealers at Coin Shows

Local, state, regional, and national coin shows are great places to buy and sell coins. Coin clubs and collector organizations frequently sponsor coin shows. Some are commercial shows, sponsored by a group of dealers or a firm that specializes in hosting and promoting shows. Dealers pay a fee for the privilege of setting up a table or booth on the coin-show bourse. (The word *bourse* is French and was used as far back as the 16th century to describe a trading exchange where items were bought and sold. In the world of coins, *bourse* is the name used for the room or hall in which coin buying and selling takes place.)

Local shows typically are held over a weekend and have fewer than 50 dealers on the bourse. Participating coin dealers are usually from within a 100-mile radius.

State and regional shows are somewhat larger, with from 100 up to 300 dealers on the bourse. State and regional shows typically attract and offer diversity in dealers and offer three to four days of buying and selling.

National coin shows typically attract more than 500 dealers. Some national shows have up to 1,200 dealers on the bourse and they buy and sell a wide range of coins and numismatic collectibles. National shows are often conducted over a four- to five-day period, but some run as long as a week.

Organizations such as the American Numismatic Association, Florida United Numismatists, and Central States Numismatic Society sponsor national shows in large cities. Some national shows are anchored in the same city year after year. Others rotate to cities in various regions of the country. Information about shows and national, regional, state, and local member clubs that also sponsor shows can be found at the ANA's web site (www.money.org). Check under "Numismatic Events" and "Coin Club Directory." Also, publications such as *Coin World* and *Numismatic News* publish weekly show calendars, online and in the print editions, that list the dates, locations, and number of tables on the coin bourse. (Go to www.coinworld.com and click on "Navigation" at the top of the home page. Scroll down to "Events" and click; this will bring up coin shows that are listed by date and location. At www.numismaticnews.net, click "Events.")

Three times per year, Whitman Coin & Collectibles Expo sponsors multiple-day conventions in Baltimore. These shows feature more than 1,300 dealers, plus educational presentations, entertaining exhibits, book signings by Whitman Publishing authors, Boy Scout Merit Badge clinics, Kids Korner, and other attractions.

Most coins shows, especially those sponsored by coin clubs, do not charge an admission fee and the shows are open to the public. When admission charges are in effect, they are modest and you can often purchase a pass that will entitle you to visit every day of the show.

Coin shows offer the opportunity to talk with many dealers, usually within the same day or within a few hours. Some dealers are "regulars" on the coin-show circuit. If you have specialized or rare coins, it may be worth attending a regional or national coin show because it provides competition that may not be present locally. Advertisers in hobby publications attend the larger coin shows. Peruse advertisements in numismatic newspapers and magazines to find dealers that advertise the kinds of coins you have for sale. Chances are they also buy those coins. By contacting the firm or checking its web site, you can ascertain whether its representatives will be attending shows within driving distance of you. You can call and talk with a representative to advise that you expect to attend the show and make an appointment to discuss your coins.

Mail-Order Coin Dealers

There are some dealerships that specialize in mail order. They advertise in numismatic and other collector publications. Some are large and employ hundreds of people who work in their fulfillment centers, which are generally not open to the public. Others are small family businesses operated in a home or small storefront and employing one or two members of the owner's family. Today, whether large or small, most mail-

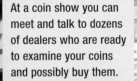

At a coin show you can meet and talk to dozens of dealers who are ready to examine your coins and possibly buy them.

order coin businesses also have web sites. They both sell and buy coins. Their primary business model is to buy and sell coins and other numismatic collectibles via mail. It is advisable to call the mail-order coin firm or check its web site to confirm that it is buying the type of coins you wish to sell. Most mail-order dealers that have web sites ask you to fill out a form listing your contact information as well as provide a list of the coins that you have for sale. If you have images of your coins, they invite you to email them with your list. If interested in buying your coins, a representative of the firm will provide a quote and instruct you regarding how to package your coins for safe shipping and a suggested shipping agent (U.S. Postal Service, UPS, FedEx, etc.). Ask the prospective mail-order buyer who is responsible for return shipping costs in case the firm, for any reason, declines to purchase your coins. Some firms will only quote a price upon being able to inspect your coins "in the flesh." Follow the firm's instructions for packaging and mailing the coins. Be sure to include in the package your name and contact information and an inventory list of what is included. A representative should contact you in a timely manner after receiving your coins, to make an offer. You do not have to accept the offer. However, if you accept the firm's offer, be sure to confirm their method of payment (usually by check) and when you can expect to receive it.

When sending coins to a mail-order firm for purchase be sure to:

- keep a copy of your list or inventory of coins sent.
- if possible, scan or take digital images of the coins you send.
- insure your coins and use a method of shipping that provides you with a way to track the package and confirm the date and delivery address.
- package your coins before going to the shipping agent's office or location. Carry your package in a bag or briefcase and do not disclose to anyone the contents of the package.
- keep your shipping receipt and tracking information handy. Track the package until it is delivered and signed for by the dealer or his representative.

SELLING COINS WITH NUMISMATIC VALUE BY PUBLIC AUCTION

If you have rare (semi-key and key date) coins with significant numismatic value, selling at public auction may offer you the opportunity to obtain the highest price, sometimes even surpassing current retail. Public auctions, especially those conducted by numismatic firms, place your coin(s) before the widest possible audience of potential buyers in a competitive environment. Both dealers and collectors bid and buy in public auctions. The larger numismatic auction firms conduct sales both online and in special venues, such as on-site in conjunction with major coin shows and conventions.

If you are seeking to sell your coins quickly, the traditional numismatic auction might not be your best choice because of the time lag between consigning your coins and receiving payment. For example, in order to benefit from the auction firm's extensive marketing and advertising of the sale, you will have to consign your coins for cataloging at least three to four months in advance of the sale. Once the coin is sold, you will likely have to wait at least another 45 days for "settlement" (being paid). Also, most numismatic auction firms charge a seller's premium, which can range from 20 percent down to 5 percent of the hammer price (the price accepted by the auctioneer as the winning bid for the coin). Most numismatic auction firms will negotiate on the seller's premium, especially if your coin is one of the marquee items in the sale or if your collection is the principal one around which the auction is built.

Most coins sold at public numismatic auctions are graded and encapsulated by the top independent, commercial grading firms. Sometimes an auction firm will submit your coin for grading and encapsulation as a part of your agreement to consign to their auctions. It is always best to contact the auction house and talk with a member of the auction consignment staff regarding coins you are considering to sell at auction. The auction firms have web sites that detail the steps in consigning and also have a copy of the auction contract you will be required to sign. Read the terms of the contract carefully and be sure you understand them. Be sure to inquire as to whether the auction house will allow you to place a minimum or reserve bid, to protect your coin from selling for an amount below what you believe to be a good price. Also, ask about any fees associated with "buy backs" or reserved bids. By visiting auction-house web sites, you can gain a good understanding of the types of coins offered in their sales. You can also peruse a firm's auction archives to check prices realized at auction for coins similar to those you wish to sell.

Following is a list some of the best-known auction firms with headquarters in the United States that specialize in numismatic collectibles, and their web sites. They are listed alphabetically.

Classical Numismatic Group, Inc.
(Specializes in classical, medieval, and British coins)
PO Box 479
Lancaster PA 17608.
Offices located in Pennsylvania and London.
www.cngcoins.com

Heritage Auctions
3500 Maple Ave.
Dallas Texas 75219.
Offices located in Dallas, New York, Beverly Hills,
    San Francisco, Paris, and Geneva.
www.ha.com

Ira and Larry Goldberg Auctioneers
11400 W. Olympic Blvd. #800
Los Angeles CA 90064.
www.goldbergcoins.com

Lyn Knight Currency Auctions
(Specializes in U.S. and world paper money)
PO Box 7364
Overland Park KS 66207.
www.lynknight.com

Stack's Bowers Galleries Coins and Currency Auctions

1063 McGaw Ave.

Irvine CA 92614.

Offices located in California, New York, New England, France, and Hong Kong.

www.stacksbowers.com

SELLING NUMISMATIC COLLECTIBLES BY ONLINE AUCTIONS

Exclusively online or Internet auctions offer faster turnarounds than traditional numismatic auctions, and some hold several auctions per week. Typically you will find popularly collected coins and paper money in these auctions. Most require that the coins or paper money be graded and encapsulated by one of the major professional independent third-party grading firms. Depending on the value of the coin being sold, it may qualify for "free" grading, meaning that the Internet auction firm may absorb the fee for having the coin graded and encapsulated. The seller's fee is based on a percentage of the price realized per coin. Generally there is a minimum standard fee for low-value items. Teletrade is the oldest exclusively online numismatic auction firm. Prior to the Internet, it conducted auctions by touch-tone phone bidding. There are other firms, such as Holabird-Kagin Americana, that conduct online auctions that are more diverse in the type of numismatic items offered.

Teletrade

1063 McGaw Ave., Suite 100

Irvine CA 92614.

www.teletrade.com

Holabird-Kagin Americana

3555 Airway Drive, Suite 308

Reno NV 89511.

www.HolabirdAmericana.com

There are many online auction firms or portals where you can buy and sell collectibles. They generally have sections for numismatic collectibles (coins, currency, tokens, medals, etc.). The largest is eBay (www.ebay.com). Large volumes of coins and numismatic collectibles, particularly lower-valued items, are sold on eBay literally every day. While you don't have to be an expert to sell coins on eBay, experienced sellers suggest that to maximize your coins' value, there are several basics to keep in mind.

Good images. For coins, it is essential that you provide images of both the obverse and reverse. Unless you have the ability to take professional-quality close-up digital images, use a good digital scanner.

Good title listings. The listing title is critical because prospective buyers use it to find your coin. By searching "completed" or "sold" listings you can learn how to write an effective title.

Accurate descriptions. It is essential to accurately describe the coin, including its grade. Review completed or sold listings for ideas on how to write a description.

Use the eBay postage system. You can use it to print your shipping labels. It automatically sends the tracking number to the buyer.

Be aware of shipping costs. Buyers on eBay generally expect free shipping for coins selling for $100 or more. However, free shipping for lower-priced coins may significantly eat into your profit. One strategy for lower-valued coins is to offer to discount shipping on multiple coins purchased by the buyer and charge only the price of the shipping, without a handling fee.

Ensure safe arrival of the coin(s). Use care in packaging coins for shipment to buyers by using padded envelopes for shipping single or a small numbers of coins. Place the coins in safe holders and wrap the holders in paper or bubble wrap. Tape the wrapped coins to the inside wall of the mailer so the coins will not shift inside the mailer during transit. If the coins can't shift, they can't escape the envelope and be lost en route to the buyer.

If you are new to eBay and are interested in delving into selling your coins there, it would pay to learn as much as you can about the process, either from an experienced eBay user or by reading postings at the site titled "Guides." Nearly 3,000 such postings have been written by users just for the Coins area (search.reviews.ebay.com/?ucat=11116&uqt=g).

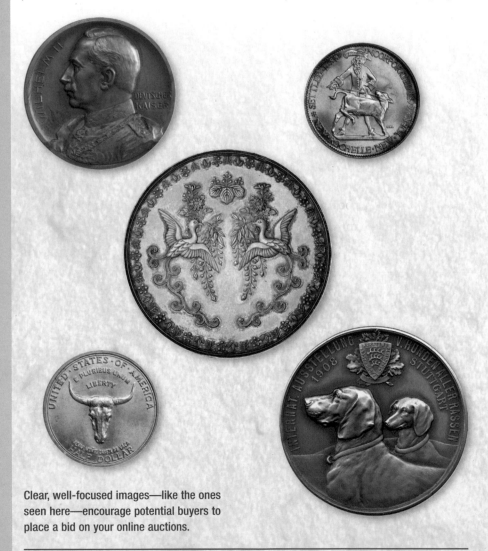

Clear, well-focused images—like the ones seen here—encourage potential buyers to place a bid on your online auctions.

Special attention is accorded eBay's Coin Grading Guide (pages.ebay .com/buy/guides/graded-coins-buying-guide). It is a must-read before you venture into selling coins at eBay.

If you are not an experienced eBay buyer or seller, one option is to use the services of an eBay Trading Assistant. Trading Assistants sell your items on eBay. The service functions like a consignment store. "Registered eBay Drop-Off Locations" (REDOLs) are storefronts with regular business hours. You can drop off your items at the store or you can arrange for someone from a REDOL to pick up items at your home or designated location. (eBay requires bonding for all REDOLs.) The Trading Assistant will examine your items for sale, prepare the listing and descriptions, and take care of shipping the sold items to the buyers. After your coins are sold, you will receive the proceeds less any fees or commissions. (eBay charges a fee, as does its subsidiary, PayPal, a payment-processing service. There are also shipping and handling costs.) It is not unusual for a Trading Assistant to charge a 40 to 50 percent commission on the gross sale. A number of people who have used the services of eBay Trading Assistants report they netted more for their coins than what they were offered by a local coin shop.

For additional information about the eBay Trading Assistant service and locations near you, visit ebaytradingassistant.com/directory/index .php?page=home.

Selling Coins for "Melt Value"

Many coins—especially common-date, lower-grade silver and gold coins—sell for "melt value."

Actually the term *selling for melt value* is a bit of a misnomer because typically coins are made of more than one metal. However, the value is often quoted in terms of the predominant metal. Let's look at an example: Washington quarters produced from 1932 through 1964 are made of 90 percent silver and 10 percent copper. So the total "melt value" would include the value of both metals. The standard weight of a silver Washington quarter is 6.25 grams. On the commodity exchanges silver is priced in terms of troy ounces. Copper is priced by the pound. Thus we must use a factor to convert each to grams. The ounce/gram conversion factor for silver is .321507466; for copper it is .00220462262.

To calculate the 90 percent silver value the formula is

price of silver per ounce × the silver conversion factor × the weight of the coin × percentage of silver = silver value

For our example we will use $19.35 per ounce as the spot price of silver:

$19.35 × .0321507466 × 6.25 × .90 = $3.49940782524375

To calculate the value of the coin's copper, the formula is

price of copper per pound × the copper conversion factor × the weight of the coin × percentage of copper = copper value

For our example we will use $3.0106 per pound as the spot price of copper:

$3.0106 × .00220462262 × 6.25 × .10 = $0.00414827303736

Add the two together:

$3.49940782524375 + $0.00414827303736 = $3.50364609828111

Thus, $3.50364609828111 is the value of the coin based on its total metal content at these prices. For practical purposes we would round this to $3.50.

However, if you contact your local coin dealer, he will likely quote you a price that will be a certain dollar amount times face value (often abbreviated and referred to in conversation as "face"). For our single Washington silver quarter, a typical price that a local dealer would quote with silver selling at $19.35 per ounce would be $13.49 × face value, which would be $13.49 × .25 = $3.37 for the silver quarter. So this dealer is actually paying 13 cents below the spot price or just over 95 percent of the value of the silver that is in coin.

The dealer's quote to you will depend on how much risk he is willing to take. Bullion prices move up and down quickly. The local dealer is likely selling either to a larger dealer who may be acquiring coins to sell in larger quantities to investors or he may be selling directly to a smelter who will be melting the coins into bars to sell in domestic and international markets. Because of the rapid transmission of data today, even some small coin shops will provide quotes multiple times during a trading day. So you need to do your homework and be aware of the spot price of the metal and estimate what the total metal value of the coins you want to sell is, compared to the dealer's quote in terms of a dollar amount × face value of your coins.

In preparation, count the number of silver or gold coins by denomination. The dealer will quote based on the denomination and the percentage of silver or gold in the coins you have for sale.

There are a number of large coin and bullion firms that buy and sell silver and gold coins based on metal content. Some have minimum quantities they will purchase. Be sure to inquire about minimums and also whether the firm will pay more if you have a large number of a particular denomination to sell. You will need to factor in shipping and handling costs when dealing with firms beyond driving distance from you.

As with coins that carry a numismatic premium, it pays to shop around. Contact several local dealers as well as larger dealers on the Internet or even smelting operations that buy directly from the public. Then calculate which is the best deal for you. Computer search engines are handy for locating dealers that buy silver and gold coins "for melt." Smelting operations that buy from the public can also be found via Internet searches.

Information about the weight and metal content of each denomination/design type is provided in the coin identification section, in chapter 5. With that information you can calculate the value of the metal content of your coins. A handy calculator of U.S. silver coins by denomination/dates of issue, weight expressed in troy ounces, and fineness of silver can be used to quickly determine values for the lower-grade, common-date coins you may have in the "sell for melt" value category.

Quick Worksheet for Silver Value of U.S. Coins

Denomination	Issue dates	Fineness	Silver weight (troy oz.)	Spot price	Silver value
Standard silver dollar	1840–1935	0.900	0.77344		
American Silver Eagle dollar	1986 to date	0.999	1.00000		
Half dollar, 90 percent silver	1873–1964	0.900	0.36169		
Half dollar, 40 percent silver	1965–1970	0.400	0.14792		
Quarter dollar	1873–1964	0.900	0.18084		
Dime	1873–1964	0.900	0.07234		
Wartime alloy 5-cent coin	1942–1945	0.350	0.05626		
$1,000 bag of silver coins	1873–1964	0.900	715.00		
$1,000 bag of 40 percent silver half dollars	1965–1970	0.400	295.00		

To calculate silver value, multiply the spot price of silver by the silver weight of the denomination.

Using the spot price of $19.35 as in the earlier example for the Washington quarter, using this chart simply multiply $19.35 × 0.18084 = $3.499254. If you have 25 silver quarters then the silver value would be $3.499254 × 25 = $87.48135. Rounded, the silver value of 25 silver (90 percent) Washington quarters would be $87.48.

If math is not your "thing," there are some helpful online calculators. The web site www.coinflation.com is free and is very useful for calculating the intrinsic or metal-content value of coins. It also shows in real time market spot prices for the metals used in coins.

Current spot prices for precious metals are available free at numismatic-publication web sites and most coin-dealer web sites. Many dealer sites link to larger precious-metals trading houses such as www.kitco.com, a comprehensive site containing live spot prices and historical prices as well as breaking news and expert market commentaries.

Historical prices of precious metals such as silver and gold may be very useful if you are required to ascertain the bullion or "melt" value of a coin on a certain date in history. For example, in valuing coins in an estate, you may be required to use the spot price of silver or gold on the date of death of the person who formed the collection. The web site www.kitco.com has an extensive section that provides historical pricing information by year, month, and date.

Selling Copper Coins Based on Metal Value

Although it is illegal to *melt* U.S. one-cent coins and five-cent coins for their metal content, it is not illegal to *sell* them based on their metal content. As the price of copper has risen in recent years, a growing trade has sprung up in bags of 95 percent copper pennies (Lincoln cents dated from 1909 through 1981). They are bought and sold in bags of various quantities. Check online auction sites such as eBay for quantities and pricing information.

LIKE-KIND TRADES

Many people who inherit coins with numismatic value are uncomfortable keeping them as an investment because of their lack of knowledge of the rare-coin market. However, they may be interested in having precious metals in their investment portfolios. Using like-kind trading allows you to transition from one to the other without incurring taxes, because no sale takes place.

For example: You have inherited a coin collection. Some of the coins have a numismatic premium and others are worth "melt" value. You have done your homework—identified your coins, created an inventory, estimated their current value, located potential buyers, and received offers to purchase. Once you confirm the amount for which you are willing to sell your coins, inquire of the buyer whether he would consider a like-kind trade for bullion coins. Many coin dealers, especially if they buy and sell bullion coins, will do a like-kind exchange of the value of your collection for an equal value in bullion coins. It is best to trade for bullion coins produced by major government mints because their precious-metal coins are recognized and traded worldwide. Some of the most popular are bullion coins produced by the U.S. Mint, the Royal

Canadian Mint, the Australian Royal Mint, the Perth Mint, the Austrian Mint, the British Royal Mint, the Mint of Mexico, and the South African Mint. You can check values of these coins daily (or hourly) because their value is based on the metal (silver, gold, or platinum).

If you transact a like-kind trade, be sure to obtain a receipt showing the value of the coins you traded for the bullion coins and the value of the bullion coins on the date of trade. The receipt will document your basis value in your bullion coins, which will be important in calculating capital gains (or losses) when you decide to sell your bullion coins.

Rare coins can be swapped for bullion in a like-kind trade to avoid taxes at the time of the transaction.

Appendix A
BULLION VALUE
OF SILVER COINS

This chart shows the bullion values of silver U.S. coins. These are *intrinsic* values and do not include any extra value collectors might give a coin because of supply and demand. The weight listed under each denomination is its actual silver weight (ASW).

In recent years the bullion price of silver has gone up and down considerably. You can use this chart to determine the approximate bullion value of many 19th- and 20th-century silver coins at various price levels—or you can calculate the approximate value by multiplying the current spot price of silver by the ASW for each coin, as indicated.

Dealers generally purchase circulated common-date silver coins at around 15 percent below bullion value, and sell them at around 15 percent above bullion value.

Silver Price Per Ounce	Wartime Nickel .05626 oz.	Dime .07234 oz.	Quarter .18084 oz.	Half Dollar .36169 oz.	Silver Clad Half Dollar .14792 oz.	Silver Dollar .77344 oz.
$13	$0.73	$0.94	$2.35	$4.70	$1.92	$10.05
14	0.79	1.01	2.53	5.06	2.07	10.83
15	0.84	1.09	2.71	5.43	2.22	11.60
16	0.90	1.16	2.89	5.79	2.37	12.38
17	0.96	1.23	3.07	6.15	2.51	13.15
18	1.01	1.30	3.26	6.51	2.66	13.92
19	1.07	1.37	3.44	6.87	2.81	14.70
20	1.13	1.45	3.62	7.23	2.96	15.47
21	1.18	1.52	3.80	7.60	3.11	16.24
22	1.24	1.59	3.98	7.96	3.25	17.02
23	1.29	1.66	4.16	8.32	3.40	17.79
24	1.35	1.74	4.34	8.68	3.55	18.56
25	1.41	1.81	4.52	9.04	3.70	19.34
26	1.46	1.88	4.70	9.40	3.85	20.11
27	1.52	1.95	4.88	9.77	3.99	20.88
28	1.58	2.03	5.06	10.13	4.14	21.66
29	1.63	2.10	5.24	10.49	4.29	22.43
30	1.69	2.17	5.43	10.85	4.44	23.20

Appendix B
BULLION VALUE
OF GOLD COINS

This chart shows the bullion values of gold U.S. coins. These are *intrinsic* values; they do not include any extra value collectors might give a coin because of supply and demand. The weight listed under each denomination is its actual gold weight (AGW).

Nearly all U.S. gold coins have an additional premium value beyond their bullion content, and thus are not affected by minor day-to-day variations in bullion price. The premium amount is not necessarily tied to the spot price of gold, but is usually determined by supply and demand levels in the numismatic marketplace. Because these factors can vary significantly, there is no reliable formula for calculating "percentage below and above bullion" prices that would remain accurate over time. This gold chart lists bullion values based on AGW only; consult a trusted coin dealer to ascertain current buy and sell prices.

Gold Price Per Ounce	$5.00 Liberty Head 1839–1908 Indian Head 1908–1929 .24187 oz.	$10.00 Liberty Head 1838–1907 Indian Head 1907–1933 .48375 oz.	$20.00 1849–1933 .96750 oz.
$1,200	$290.24	$580.50	$1,161.00
1,225	296.29	592.59	1,185.19
1,250	302.34	604.69	1,209.38
1,275	308.38	616.78	1,233.56
1,300	314.43	628.88	1,257.75
1,325	320.48	640.97	1,281.94
1,350	326.52	653.06	1,306.13
1,375	332.57	665.16	1,330.31
1,400	338.62	677.25	1,354.50
1,425	344.66	689.34	1,378.69
1,450	350.71	701.44	1,402.88
1,475	356.76	713.53	1,427.06
1,500	362.81	725.63	1,451.25
1,525	368.85	737.72	1,475.44
1,550	374.90	749.81	1,499.63
1,575	380.95	761.91	1,523.81

BIBLIOGRAPHY

This is a list of recommended recent books that cover specific U.S. coin series and general related history. This is only a fraction of the standard references available to today's collectors; for a more detailed list, consult the bibliography in the back of the most recent edition of the *Guide Book of United States Coins*.

COLONIAL ISSUES

Bowers, Q. David. *Whitman Encyclopedia of Colonial and Early American Coins*, Atlanta, GA, 2009.

SMALL CENTS

Bowers, Q. David. *A Guide Book of Lincoln Cents*, Atlanta, GA, 2008.

Snow, Richard. *A Guide Book of Flying Eagle and Indian Head Cents* (2nd ed.), Atlanta, GA, 2009.

NICKEL FIVE-CENT PIECES

Bowers, Q. David. *A Guide Book of Buffalo and Jefferson Nickels*, Atlanta, GA, 2007.

Bowers, Q. David. *A Guide Book of Shield and Liberty Head Nickels*, Atlanta, GA, 2006.

DIMES

Flynn, Kevin. *The Authoritative Reference on Roosevelt Dimes*, Brooklyn, NY, 2001.

Greer, Brian. *The Complete Guide to Liberty Seated Dimes*, Virginia Beach, VA, 2005.

Lange, David W. *The Complete Guide to Mercury Dimes* (2nd ed.), Virginia Beach, VA, 2005.

Lawrence, David. *The Complete Guide to Barber Dimes*, Virginia Beach, VA, 1991.

QUARTER DOLLARS

Bowers, Q. David. *A Guide Book of Washington and State Quarters*, Atlanta, GA, 2006.

Briggs, Larry. *The Comprehensive Encyclopedia of United States Seated Quarters*, Lima, OH, 1991.

Cline, J.H. *Standing Liberty Quarters* (3rd ed.), 1996.

Lawrence, David. *The Complete Guide to Barber Quarters*, Virginia Beach, VA, 1989.

Rea, Rory, Peterson, Glenn, Karoleff, Bradley, and Kovach, John. *Early Quarter Dollars of the U.S. Mint, 1796–1838*. 2010.

HALF DOLLARS

Ambio, Jeff. *Collecting and Investing Strategies for Walking Liberty Half Dollars*, Irvine, CA, 2008.

Flynn, Kevin. *The Authoritative Reference on Barber Half Dollars*, Brooklyn, NY, 2005.

Tomaska, Rick. *A Guide Book of Franklin and Kennedy Half Dollars* (2nd ed.), Atlanta, GA, 2012.

Wiley, Randy, and Bugert, Bill. *The Complete Guide to Liberty Seated Half Dollars*, Virginia Beach, VA, 1993.

SILVER DOLLARS

Bowers, Q. David. *A Guide Book of Morgan Silver Dollars: A Complete History and Price Guide* (4th ed.), Atlanta, GA, 2012.

Burdette, Roger W. *A Guide Book of Peace Dollars* (2nd ed.), Atlanta, GA, 2012.

Newman, Eric P., and Bressett, Kenneth E. *The Fantastic 1804 Dollar: Tribute Edition*, Atlanta, GA, 2009.

GOLD PIECES ($1 THROUGH $20)

Bowers, Q. David. *A Guide Book of Double Eagle Gold Coins*, Atlanta, GA, 2004.

Bowers, Q. David. *A Guide Book of Gold Dollars*, Atlanta, GA, 2008.

Fivaz, Bill. *United States Gold Counterfeit Detection Guide*, Atlanta, GA, 2005.

Garrett, Jeff, and Guth, Ron. *Encyclopedia of U.S. Gold Coins, 1795–1933* (2nd ed.), Atlanta, GA, 2008.

Moran, Michael. *Striking Change: The Great Artistic Collaboration Between Theodore Roosevelt and Augustus Saint-Gaudens*, Atlanta, GA, 2008.

SILVER, GOLD, AND PLATINUM BULLION

Bowers, Q. David, and Garrett, Jeff. *Gold: Everything You Need to Know to Buy and Sell Today*, Atlanta, GA, 2010.

Mercanti, John M., and Standish, Michael "Miles." *American Silver Eagles: A Guide to the U.S. Bullion Coin Program*, Atlanta, GA, 2012.

Moy, Edmund C. *American Gold and Platinum Eagles*, Atlanta, GA, 2013.

Tucker, Dennis. *American Gold and Silver: U.S. Mint Collector and Investor Coins and Medals, Bicentennial to Date*, Atlanta, GA, 2014.

COMMEMORATIVES

Bowers, Q. David. *A Guide Book of United States Commemorative Coins*, Atlanta, GA, 2008.

Swiatek, Anthony J. *Encyclopedia of the Commemorative Coins of the United States*, Chicago, IL, 2012.

WORLD COINS

Yeoman, R.S., revised and edited by Arthur L. Friedberg. *A Catalog of Modern World Coins, 1850–1964* (14th ed.), Atlanta, GA, 2008.

PROOF COINS AND PROOF SETS

Lange, David W. *A Guide Book of Modern United States Proof Coin Sets* (2nd ed.), Atlanta, GA, 2010.

TYPE COINS

Bowers, Q. David. *A Guide Book of United States Type Coins* (2nd ed.), Atlanta, GA, 2008.

Garrett, Jeff, and Guth, Ron. *100 Greatest U.S. Coins* (4th ed.), Atlanta, GA, 2014.

Guth, Ron, and Garrett, Jeff. *United States Coinage: A Study by Type*, Atlanta, GA, 2005.

Tucker, Dennis B. (editor). *Almanac of United States Coins*, Atlanta, GA, 2013.

Yeoman, R.S., edited by Kenneth Bressett. *A Guide Book of United States Coins*, Atlanta, GA, published annually.

GRADING U.S. COINS

Bowers, Q. David. *Grading Coins by Photographs: An Action Guide for the Collector and Investor* (2nd ed.), Atlanta, GA, 2012.

Bressett, Kenneth (editor). *The Official American Numismatic Association Grading Standards for United States Coins* (7th ed.), Atlanta, GA, 2013.

Deisher, Beth. *Making the Grade: A Comprehensive Grading Guide to U.S. Coins* (3rd ed.), Sydney, OH, 2012.

HISTORY OF THE U.S. MINT

Augsburger, Leonard D., and Orosz, Joel J. *The Secret History of the First U.S. Mint.* Atlanta, GA, 2011.

Lange, David W. *History of the United States Mint and Its Coinage*, Atlanta, GA, 2005.

Lee, Karen M. *The Private Sketchbook of George T. Morgan, America's Silver Dollar Artist*, Atlanta, GA, 2013.

ABOUT THE AUTHOR AND ACKNOWLEDGMENTS

Beth Deisher for 27 years was editor of *Coin World*, the world's largest and most widely circulated news weekly specializing in coverage of collectible coins, medals, paper money, exonumia, and any item once used as money. She joined *Coin World* in 1981 as news editor and also served as executive editor before being tapped to lead the editorial team in 1985.

A graduate of the University of North Carolina at Greensboro, Deisher began her career as a feature writer, communications specialist, and newspaper journalist before joining *Coin World*. She was founding editor of three numismatic magazines—*Coin Values*, *Paper Money Values*, and *WorldWide Coins*—and primary author of *Making the Grade: A Comprehensive Grading Guide to U.S. Coins*. She supervised updates of five editions of the *Coin World Almanac*, and was founding editor of *Coin World's Guide to U.S. Coins, Prices & Value Trends*.

Deisher is a Fellow of the American Numismatic Society and holds memberships in many state, regional and national numismatic organizations, including the American Numismatic Association. She is the recipient of numerous awards for her work within the hobby community. She was inducted into the Numismatic Hall of Fame in 2013.

Outside of numismatics, Deisher has provided leadership in professional organizations including as president of Ohio Professional Writers. In 40-plus years as a member of the National Federation of Press Women she has been recognized three times on the national level as a Communicator of Achievement. She is also a 43-year member of the Society of Professional Journalists. She and her husband live in Ohio.

Credits and Acknowledgements

The author expresses appreciation to the following for help in the ways indicated: Q. David Bowers, for many years of advice and wise counsel, and for writing the foreword to this book. Dr. Gregory V. DuBay, for sharing his knowledge about counterfeits of U.S. coins made in China, and for loaning coins and albums of counterfeits from his collection for photography. Joel J. Forman, accredited senior appraiser with a specialty in numismatics, American Society of Appraisers, for information about numismatic appraisals. Steve Roach, accredited appraiser and member of the board of directors of the International Society of Appraisers, for information about best practices and elements of a competent appraisal report. Jimmy Hayes, former member of Congress and legislative consultant to the Industry Council for Tangible Assets, for assistance in researching the new tax laws approved in early January 2013 and for helping to decipher their applicability to numismatic collectibles. Dr. Rita Laws, for advice and information about selling coins and other numismatic collectibles on eBay. Linda Pizzuto, for the loan of coins for photography. Margo Russell, for numismatic mentoring and many years of advice and wise counsel. The staff of Whitman Publishing, for their hard work on this book.

Whitman Publishing would like to thank the American Numismatic Association, the American Numismatic Society, the Library of Congress, Leonard Opanashuk, Stack's Bowers Galleries, Michael Tucker, and the U.S. Mint for providing images; and Brent Cook for photography. Some images were reproduced, with permission, from the *Guide Book of United States Coins*; *Grading Coins by Photographs*; *American Silver Eagles*, and other Whitman books. Some photographs are of the collection of Bernard Heller. The counterfeit Morgan dollar in chapter 8 is from the Dr. Gregory V. DuBay Collection of Chinese-Made Counterfeits. In chapter 10, the photograph of the widow's mite fresco (from the Basilika Ottobeuren) is courtesy of Johannes Böckh and Thomas Mirtsch. The publisher would like to thank the coin collectors, dealers, and other readers of the first edition of this book, for sharing their feedback and enthusiasm.

INDEX

On page 169, the 1885-S "coin" on top is a fake.